ECONOMIC AND SOCIAL COMMISSION FOR ASIA AND THE PACIFIC

STATISTICAL PROFILES   No. 12

WOMEN IN INDIA

A COUNTRY PROFILE

UNITED NATIONS

New York, 1997

DBW: 1658296

ST/ESCAP/1765

UNITED NATIONS PUBLICATION

Sales No. E.97.II.F.24

ISBN 92-1-119760-0

UN2

ST/ESCAP/1765

The views expressed in this profile are those of the author and do not necessarily reflect those of the United Nations. The designations employed and the presentation of the material in this publication do not imply the expression of any opinion whatsoever on the part of the Secretariat of the United Nations concerning the legal status of any country, territory, city or area, or of its authorities, or concerning the delimitation of its frontiers or boundaries. Mention of firm names and commercial products does not imply the endorsement of the United Nations.

The profile has been prepared under project BK-X20-3-214, on improving statistics on women in the ESCAP region.

FOREWORD

The call for the development of statistics and indicators on the situation of women has, for some time, been voiced in various global and regional forums. It was first recommended by the World Plan of Action for the Implementation of the Objectives of the International Women's Year, adopted in 1975. The recommendations of the World Plan of Action were reaffirmed and elaborated in the Programme of Action for the Second Half of the United Nations Decade for Women: Equality, Development and Peace. On various occasions, the Commission, stressing the importance of social and human development, has recognized the need for improved statistics and indicators on women. It has noted that better indicators are required to monitor the situation of women and to assess the effectiveness of strategies and programmes designed to address priority gender issues.

The secretariat initiated the project on improving statistics on women in the ESCAP region in 1994. The project aims to support governments in their efforts to promote the full integration of women in development and improve their status in line with the Nairobi Forward-looking Strategies for the Advancement of Women adopted in 1985. The project has been implemented by the Economic and Social Commission for Asia and the Pacific (ESCAP) through its subprogramme on statistics, with funding assistance from the Government of the Netherlands.

As a major component of its activities, the project commissioned experts from 19 countries in the region to prepare country profiles on the situation of women and men in the family, at work, and in public life, by analysing available statistical data and information. The profiles are intended to highlight the areas where action is needed, and to raise the consciousness of readers about issues concerning women and men. The 19 countries are Bangladesh, China, India, Indonesia, the Islamic Republic of Iran, Japan, Nepal, Pakistan, the Philippines, the Republic of Korea, Sri Lanka and Thailand in Asia; and Cook Islands, Fiji, Papua New Guinea, Samoa, Solomon Islands, Tonga and Vanuatu in the Pacific.

The secretariat hosted two meetings each in Asia and in the Pacific as part of the project activities. In the first meeting, the experts discussed and agreed on the structure, format and contents of the country profiles, based on guidelines prepared by the secretariat through Ms C.N. Ericta, consultant. The second meeting was a workshop to review the draft profiles. Participants in the workshop included the country experts and invited representatives from national statistical offices of Brunei Darussalam, Hong Kong, the Lao People's Democratic Republic, Mongolia and Viet Nam in Asia; of Marshall Islands, Tuvalu, and Vanuatu in the Pacific; and representatives of United Nations organizations, specialized agencies and international organizations.

The original draft of the present profile, *Women in India,* was prepared by Mr Anil Baran Bose, Professor, Indira Gandhi National Open University. It was technically edited and modified by the ESCAP secretariat with the assistance of Mr S. Selvaratnam, consultant. The profiles express the views of the authors and not necessarily those of the secretariat.

I wish to express my sincere appreciation to the Government of the Netherlands for its generous financial support, which enabled the secretariat to implement the project.

Adrianus Mooy
Executive Secretary

iii

CONTENTS

LIST OF TABLES

LIST OF TABLES *(continued)*

LIST OF TABLES *(continued)*

LIST OF FIGURES

LIST OF ANNEX TABLES

LIST OF ANNEX TABLES *(continued)*

PART I

DESCRIPTIVE ANALYSIS

INTRODUCTION

The principle of gender equality and gender equity has been basic to traditional Indian thinking and the Hindu religious philosophy. This is more than amplified by the religious dualism or the deification of male and female gods. Indeed, a plethora of goddesses continue to occupy pivotal places in Indian mythology. The concept of woman as *Sakthi*, the primal energy force, finds expression in the famous epic *Mahabaratha*, which exalts woman as a "light of the house, mother of the universe and supporter of the earth and all its forests". Various research studies also testify that during the Vedic period, women participated fully in the religious rituals, enjoyed freedom of movement, had the same rights and access to education as men, married later and had a say in the choice of their marriage partners.

Over the years, however, the honoured position that women enjoyed in the family and society began to undergo radical changes, particularly since the pronouncement by Manu, the Hindu law-giver, regarding a woman's changing position through her life cycle: "In childhood subject to her father, in youth to her husband, and when her husband is dead to her sons, she should never enjoy independence ...". The imagery of woman created by the Hindu lore thus became paradoxical and contradictory; on the one hand she was hailed as the embodiment of purity and spiritual power, and on the other she was treated as an essentially weak and dependent creature needing the constant guardianship and protection of man. Marriage, motherhood and service to the husband came to be regarded as the most valuable attributes of women, and in course of time inhuman "traditions" such as child marriage, the dowry system, purdah, or seclusion of women, and *sati*, or the immolation of the widow on the dead husband's pyre, came to be piled against women.

Despite the various socio-cultural handicaps, Indian women have played a very active role in the economic, social and political development of their country. During the nineteenth and twentieth centuries, a succession of women's movements were engaged, initially, in burning social issues such as women's education and widow remarriage, and subsequently in the national freedom struggle itself. The increasing involvement of women in social and political transformation was facilitated by the pronouncements of Mahatma Gandhi, the chief architect of the country's Freedom Movement. According to Gandhi, freedom of the nation was the sum total of the freedom of all individuals, and "woman is the companion of man gifted with equal mental capacities ... and she has the same right of freedom and liberty as he". Nevertheless, in India, for various reasons, women have not been accorded equality of status with men in almost all aspects of social, cultural, economic and political life.

The profound concern with the rights and status of women and the recognition of the need to bring women into the mainstream of development have underpinned national policy and planning since independence. The Constitution of India, adopted in 1950, guarantees fundamental rights to all citizens; article 14 confers equal rights and opportunities on men and women in political, economic and social spheres. Article 15, while prohibiting any discrimination on grounds of religion, race, caste, sex, descent or place of birth, provides a clause that empowers the State to adopt measures of affirmative discrimination in favour of women to neutralize the cumulative socio-economic, educational and political disabilities faced by them. The Constitution further imposes a fundamental duty on every citizen to uphold the dignity of women.

A major initiative in the direction of enhancing the status of women in India was the establishment in 1953 of the Central Social Welfare Board (CSWB), an apex organization at the national level, to undertake a number of welfare measures through the voluntary sector. Beginning from the Second Five-year Plan (1956-1961), the Government promoted and supported the establishment of *Mahila Mandals*, or women's groups at the grass-roots level, to ensure better implementation of welfare schemes. In the subsequent third, fourth and interim plans covering the period 1961 to 1974, priority was accorded to enhancing women's education and improving maternal and child health services.

Several legislative measures (including the Suppression of Immoral Traffic in Women and Girls Act 1956, the Hindu Succession Act 1956, and the Dowry Prohibition Act 1961) were also undertaken to protect the interests of women. By and large, the main approach was to view women as beneficiaries of social services rather than as contributors to development.

However, women were brought to the forefront of development concerns during the 1970s with the appointment in 1971 of the Committee on Status of Women in India (CSWI), and the publication in 1975 of its comprehensive report entitled "Towards Equality"; the action that followed included the setting up of an Inter-Ministerial Empowered Committee to process the recommendations of CSWI; the constitution in 1974 of a high-powered national committee under the chairmanship of the Prime Minister for the observance of International Women's Year; and the formulation of a National Plan of Action for Women in 1975-1976. A visible national machinery for women's development came into formal existence in 1976 with the setting up of the Women's Bureau in the Department of Social Welfare (Government of India). A large number of non-governmental organizations and academicians were activated, and centres for women's studies came into existence in several universities. The 1970s also witnessed the enactment of important specific legislation such as the Equal Remuneration Act 1976, as well as amendments to various labour laws to safeguard the interests of women and provide for their welfare.

The Sixth Five-year Plan (1980-1985) adopted a multidisciplinary approach to women's development with a three-pronged thrust on health, education and employment. For the first time in India's planning history, women's development received recognition as a specific development sector with a separate chapter on women and development included in the Sixth Plan. In the Seventh Plan (1985-1990), development programmes for women were continued with the objective of enhancing their socio-economic status and bringing them into the mainstream of national development. The National Perspective Plan for Women (1988-2000)

provides directions for the all-round development of women.

Another important development during the 1980s was the setting up at the national level of a separate Department of Women and Child Development in 1985 within the newly created Ministry of Human Resources Development. Subsequently, many new institutions have emerged to interact with and add on to the existing network. Women's Cells were set up in the Central Ministries and Departments of Labour, Industry, Rural Development, Science and Technology to look after women's development concerns in various sectors. A high-level statutory body, the National Commission for Women (NCW), was set up in January 1992 to oversee the implementation of constitutional and legal safeguards and the protection of women's rights and privileges. The various states have also set up their own statutory state commissions for women.

At the national level, the Department of Women and Child Development acts as the machinery within government to guide, coordinate and review the efforts of both governmental and non-governmental organizations. The Central Social Welfare Board (CSWB) acts as an umbrella organization networking through state welfare boards and, through them, thousands of voluntary organizations. The National Institute of Public Cooperation and Child Development (NIPCCD) assists the Department of Women and Child Development in areas of research and training (figure 1).

Over the years, strenuous efforts have been made towards mainstreaming women into the national development process by enhancing their socio-economic, legal and political status. In addition to the general development programmes, a number of supplementary schemes were implemented by the Department of Women and Child Development. Grants were given to voluntary organizations to promote and support women's development. The schemes of condensed courses of education and vocational training for adult women were expanded to provide continuing education and training to school dropouts and improve their chances of employment. Women's development corporations have already

Figure 1. National machinery for women's development in India

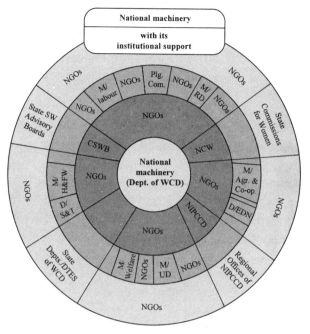

CSWB	= Central Social Welfare Board
Dept. of WCD	= Department of Women and Child Development
D/EDN	= Department of Education
D/S&T	= Department of Science and Technology
M/Agr. & Co-op.	= Ministry of Agriculture and Cooperatives
M/H&FW	= Ministry of Health and Family Welfare
M/Labour	= Ministry of Labour
M/RD	= Ministry of Rural Development
M/UD	= Ministry of Urban Development
M/Welfare	= Ministry of Welfare
NCW	= National Commission of Women
NIPCCD	= National Institute of Public Cooperation and Child Development
Plg. Com.	= Planning Commission
SW	= Social Welfare

Source: Government of India, *Fourth World Conference on Women, Beijing, 1995: Country Report,* Department of Women and Child Development, Ministry of Human Resources Development.

been set up in 12 states to promote economic activities, organize training and generate employment. Assistance was given to voluntary organizations to set up production units to provide work and wages to poor women. In 1993, the National Credit Fund for Women, "Rashtriya Mahila Kosh", was established to help develop a national network of credit services for women in order to boost self-employment, micro-enterprises and small businesses.

Legal Literacy Manuals, written in a simple and illustrated format, were published by the government in 1992. These manuals, which cover a wide range of subjects, such as laws relating to working women, child labour, contract labour, adoption and maintenance, and Hindu, Muslim and Christian marriage laws, including

rights to property and dowry issues, are intended to educate women about the laws concerning their basic rights. The 73rd and 74th Constitutional Amendments effected in 1993 guarantee women a minimum one-third representation in all local bodies in both the rural and urban areas, and also reserve one third of all posts of chairpersons for women.

On account of the general and special educational, health and economic programmes and initiatives undertaken in various parts of the country, the progress made during the past two decades in enhancing the status of women has been noteworthy. As will be noted in subsequent sections of this profile, significant gains have been achieved in areas relating to women's rights, education, employment and health. There has been a distinct orientation in favour of women's equality and empowerment and consequently a greater awareness and understanding of rights and responsibilities. An increasing number of women are participating in the education system and women's literary rates have increased substantially over the past few decades. Today, Indian women have expanded access to needed health services; female life expectancy at birth has risen dramatically and almost equals that of men. There has also been a marked rise in female employment and work participation.

Despite the commendable achievements and progress made, gender discrimination and gender disparities still persist in several areas. For example, women continue to lag behind men in regard to education, literacy, health and employment, and constitute the majority of persons living in absolute poverty. By and large, women are excluded from decision-making structures and processes at all levels: government, corporate, societal and household. Violence against women, both societal and domestic, continues unabated. Concerted efforts are therefore needed in these and other areas in order to ensure equality of opportunity for women.

The formulation and implementation of appropriate policies and programmes to enhance the status of women in the country require accurate and up-to-date data and information.

In other words, databases should be developed around women's issues and concerns to provide specific information to researchers, planners and policy makers at all levels. Fortunately, there is now a conscious effort on the part of statistical agencies and the relevant ministries/departments to present data disaggregated by gender. This will help to obtain a clear and comprehensive picture of the current situation as well as to identify areas for further action. It is hoped that the present profile will serve as a model for the compilation and analysis of gender-disaggregated data and be useful to planners, policy makers and researchers interested in women's development.

A. HIGHLIGHTS

The setting

1. With a total land area of approximately 3.3 million square kilometres, India is the seventh largest country in the world. The Indian subcontinent is characterized by a variety of physical features as well as by a great diversity of climate.

2. India is a union of states comprising 25 states and 6 union territories and the National Capital Territory of Delhi, with the President as the Head of the Union. However, the day-to-day administration of the country is the responsibility of the Cabinet, headed by a Prime Minister. The political and administrative structure at the level of the states is similar to that of the Union.

3. The population of the country, as enumerated at the latest census held in March 1991, was 846.3 million. In terms of population size, India ranks second in the world next to China. The population is unevenly distributed across the various states, with the largest concentration in Uttar Pradesh State. India is predominantly a rural country, with only about 26 per cent of its people living in areas defined as urban.

4. India is a multi-linguistic, multi-religious and multi-caste country. The 225 languages spoken in the country belong to two great language families: Indo-Aryan, mainly spoken in the north,

and Dravidian, mainly spoken in the south. While Hinduism is the religion of the majority, there is a substantial number of Moslems, Christians, Sikhs, Zorastians, Buddhists, Jains and Jews. Indian society is also divided into numerous castes, each of which is endogamous and into one of which a person enters irrevocably at birth.

5. Despite being the world's sixth biggest economy in terms of purchasing power, India is one of the poorest countries in the world. Agriculture and allied industries constitute the most important sector, contributing about a third of the gross domestic product (GDP) and absorbing about 70 per cent of the national workforce. Although the incidence of poverty is estimated to have declined in recent years, a fifth of the population is deemed to be below the poverty line.

6. Since independence, India has made considerable progress in expanding the education system and health services. While educational enrolments and literacy rates have recorded dramatic progress over the years, there are still a large number of children who lack access to educational facilities, and literacy rates are still low compared with several other developing countries.

7. Expansion of health infrastructure and services has resulted in considerable reductions in the incidence of morbidity and mortality. Nevertheless, health standards are generally poor, particularly in the rural areas.

Women's profile

1. Successive census enumerations have shown that in India, as in several other developing countries, males outnumber females in the total population. According to the 1991 census, females constituted about 48 per cent of the population; in other words, there were about 93 females for every 100 males. This deficit has been attributed to several factors, such as sex-differential enumeration, male-favoured sex ratio at birth, and higher female than male mortality.

2. A little over 47 per cent of females compared with 46 per cent of males are below 20

years of age. The proportion of women in reproductive ages 15-49 increased from 46.7 per cent in 1970 to 50.9 per cent in 1992.

3. Among persons aged 10 years and over, a significantly higher proportion of females compared with males were reported to be currently married at various censuses. The proportion of the population living in a state of marital disruption (widowed, divorced/separated) is also higher among females than males.

4. Despite intensive efforts during the past four decades, females lag behind males in regard to educational participation as well as educational attainment. Enrolment ratios for girls are substantially lower than for boys at the middle and higher levels of education. The drop-out rate, which is also considerably higher among females, continues to be a major problem, with nearly 40 per cent of girls enrolling at the primary stage dropping out before completing this level, and about 57 per cent dropping out before completing upper primary levels.

5. About 61 per cent of the 320.4 million persons reported as illiterate in 1991 were women. The female illiteracy rate (39.3 per cent) is among the lowest in the region. There are also marked regional disparities in the female literacy rate, ranging from a low of about 21 per cent in Rajasthan to near-universal literacy in Kerala.

6. Although increasing attention has been paid to enhancing the health status of women, available studies indicate that, for various reasons, females use existing health services and facilities to a lesser extent than males. The nutritional status of girls and women is generally lower than that of boys and men, and undernutrition and malnutrition are a more serious problem among poor women, pregnant women and lactating mothers.

7. Nevertheless, the overall death rate of females has declined significantly during the past two decades. While age-specific death rates for females declined for all age groups, female death rates are higher than male rates up to the age group 25-29. The estimated maternal mortality rate of 437 per 100,000 live births is about 50 times higher than that for developed countries.

8. Female life expectancy at birth has increased steadily over the years, reaching 58.1 years in 1986-1990 compared with 57.7 years for males.

Women in family life

1. The traditional joint family is gradually being replaced by the nuclear family. In 1981, nuclear-type households constituted about 54 per cent of all households in the country. However, the average household increased from 4.9 members in 1951 to 5.7 in 1992/93.

2. Female-headed households account for only a tenth of all households in the country. This proportion is higher in rural than in urban areas, and varies significantly across the states.

3. Significant changes are taking place in regard to marriage customs, practices and patterns throughout the country. An increasing number of marriages are being contracted by the couples themselves instead of being arranged by the parents, as was the tradition. There is also an increasing trend among women to refrain from early marriage but enter into marital union at a later stage.

4. The singulate mean age at marriage for females has been rising from about 13 years in 1901 to 18.4 years in 1981 and further to 20.0 years in 1992/93. Females tend to marry men who are about five years older than themselves. Despite these changes, early marriages and child marriages are still prevalent in certain areas of India.

5. During the past two decades, there have also been significant changes in the reproductive behaviour and patterns of Indian women, as indicated by a decline in the crude birth rate from 36.8 per thousand population in 1970 to 28.7 in 1990-1992, and in the total fertility rate from 5.3 children per woman to 3.4 children per woman during the same period. Today, an average Indian mother gives birth to about two children fewer than her counterpart two decades ago.

7

6. The decline in fertility has largely been due to the increasing practice of contraception among married couples. The contraceptive prevalence rate has increased more than fourfold, from 10.4 per cent in 1970/71 to 45.4 per cent in 1993/94.

7. Although the contraceptive prevalence rate in India is comparatively lower than the rates in several other countries of the region, a 1992/93 National Family Health Survey revealed that a very high proportion (96 per cent) of ever-married as well as currently married women know about at least one method of contraception and that 85 per cent of them know where to obtain at least one method of family planning.

8. The age-specific fertility rates have declined for women in all age groups, but the decline was small for the peak fertility ages 20-24 and more significant for the age groups above 30 years.

9. Recent surveys also indicate that the majority of births (more than 50 per cent) occurring in the country every year are first and second order births and that the median birth interval is 32 months.

10. The average number of children for an Indian woman also varies markedly across the states, ranging from less than 2.1 in seven states (Kerala, Andhra Pradesh, Karnataka, Tamil Nadu, Goa, Maharashtra and Gujarat) to more than four in Madhya Pradesh, Haryana, Bihar, Arunachal Pradesh and Uttar Pradesh.

11. The proportion of women living in a state of marital disruption is relatively low, with about 3.1 per cent of all females aged 15-49 years being widowed and another 1.6 per cent being either divorced or separated, according to the 1992/93 National Family Health Survey.

Women in economic life

1. Although women constitute an important segment of the national labour force, their contribution to the economy has not been adequately accounted for in the labour force statistics. The existing methods of measuring economic activity had rendered invisible much of the work performed by women.

2. According to the 1991 census data, only about 23 per cent of the women as against 52 per cent of the men were reckoned to be economically active, the activity rate for rural women (27.2 per cent) being nearly three times that for urban women (9.7 per cent).

3. A considerably higher proportion of women workers (28 per cent) compared with male workers (2 per cent) are marginal workers or those who work for less than six months during the year. In 1991, women constituted 90 per cent of all marginal workers in the country.

4. There were changes in the pattern of activity of female main workers between 1981 and 1991, with the proportion of cultivators increasing from 33 to more than 34 per cent and the proportion of labourers declining from 46 to 45 per cent. During this period, the proportion of female main workers engaged in the household manufacturing industry also decreased, from 4.6 to 3.5 per cent.

5. Woman's employment in the organized sector has increased significantly, from about 1.9 million in 1970 to 4.0 million in 1993. Nearly 62 per cent of organized sector women employees are now employed in the public sector.

6. Data from various sources also indicate that about 75 per cent of all urban women workers are employed in the informal sector, and that migrants from rural areas constitute a substantial proportion of urban female informal workers.

7. There are significant differences in the average earnings of male and female workers. In general, the wages received by women are considerably lower than those received by men, particularly in the agricultural sector.

8. Available data also point to a considerably higher unemployment rate for urban females (4.7 per cent) compared with rural females (0.3 per cent). The number of women on the live register of the employment exchanges has also been rising in recent years.

Women in public life

1. With the granting of equal voting rights after independence, an increasing number of women have participated in the political process voters, candidates contesting elections, and elected members in the National Parliament, as well as in state legislative assemblies.

2. However, no serious efforts have so far been made to mobilize women as a political constituency. Political parties are still reluctant to field women candidates, and consequently women are very much underrepresented in the legislature at both the national and state levels.

3. The representation of women in the grass-roots-level institutions of government has been considerably enhanced consequent to the 73rd Constitutional Amendment effected in 1993, whereby one third of the total number of seats in these institutions is reserved for women.

4. Women are also grossly underrepresented in the country's two premier civil services, the Indian Administrative Service and the Indian Foreign Service, although the number of women recruited to these services has been increasing over the years. In 1992, less than 4 per cent of the High Court judges were women, and there was no woman among the Supreme Court judges.

5. The proportion of women in the total number of teachers at all levels of education has been increasing steadily during the past four decades.

Special concerns

1. There is an increase in various types of crimes against women, such as rape, kidnapping and abduction, molestation, torture, and sexual harassment. More than 80 per cent of rape victims are women under 30 years of age.

2. The incidence of suicide among women is less than among men and the most important single cause of suicide among both males and females is suffering from some dreadful disease. Domestic quarrels are a more significant cause of suicide among females than males.

B. THE SETTING

1. Geography

The Republic of India stretches between latitudes 8°4 and 37°6 N and longitudes 68°7 and 97°25 E. It is bounded by China, Nepal and Bhutan in the north; Pakistan and the Arabian Sea in the west; Sri Lanka and the Indian Ocean in the south; and the Bay of Bengal, Bangladesh and Myanmar in the east. The total land area of the country is 3,287,263 square kilometres, which constitutes about 2.4 per cent of the earth's land surface. In terms of area, India is the seventh largest country in the world.

India is characterized by a variety of physical features, such as mountains, hills, plateaux and plains which could be grouped into three broad relief regions: the mountain wall of the Himalayas and associated mountains, stretching across northern India from west to east with an array of peaks mostly over 6,100 metres; the Great Plains, stretching from west to east and encompassing an area of about 840,000 square kilometres; and Peninsular India or Deccan, covering about two fifths of the country to the south.

The entire subcontinent is drained by 14 major river systems and nearly 100 medium and minor river systems. The rivers that originate from the Himalayas are perennial and are also prone to flooding during the monsoon months. The peninsular rivers originating at relatively low altitudes are mostly rainfed.

India has a great diversity of climates, ranging from sub-freezing winters in the Himalayas to year-round tropical climates in the southern tip of the peninsula; and from the damp rainy climate of Assam and Bengal in the east to the aridity of the Thar desert in the west.

2. Government

India is a union of states comprising 32 subnational units: 25 states, 6 union territories and the National Capital Territory of Delhi. The Head of the Union is the President, in whom all executive power is vested. In practice, however, and under the provisions of the Constitution, the President functions under the advice of the Cabinet headed by the Prime Minister. It is thus the Cabinet which conducts all the affairs of the government in the name of the President. The Prime Minister, who is the elected leader of the majority party in the Lok Sabha, is the supreme political leader of the nation.

The Parliament of the Union consists of the President, the Council of States (Rajya Sabha) and the House of People (Lok Sabha). The political and administrative structure at the level of the states closely resembles that of the Union. The Governor, appointed by the President, is the head of the executive branch, but the principal decision-making power lies with the Council of Ministers headed by the Chief Minister. Some states have bicameral legislatures, while others have only one house. Each union territory is administered directly by the President acting through an Administrator appointed by him. There is a strict division between the activities handled by the Union and by the states based on the accepted principle that matters which for convenience and efficiency ought to be administered on an all-India basis are vested in the Union government, while other matters can conveniently be administered by the state governments.

For administrative convenience, each state is divided into a number of districts, each under a Collector/District Magistrate who is responsible for the collection of revenue, the maintenance of law and order, and for developmental activities of the district. The administrative units below the district level are generally known as *tahsils* in northern states, *taluks* in southern states, and subdivisions/community development blocks/police stations in the eastern states and union territories.

Geographically, Madhya Pradesh is the largest state, accounting for 13.5 per cent of the total area of the country, followed by Rajasthan, Maharashtra, Uttar Pradesh and Andhra Pradesh. The smaller states comprise Tripura, Nagaland, Manipur, Meghalaya and Sikkim.

3. Population growth and distribution

The population of India has been enumerated at 13 decennial censuses, starting in 1871. According to the last census, held in March 1991, the population of the country numbered 846.3 million. In terms of population size, India ranks second in the world, next to China. India's population, as recorded at the various censuses held during this century, together with percentage decadal variation and average annual growth rates, are shown in table 1.

Table 1. Population growth: 1901-1991

Census year	Enumerated population	Percentage decadal change	Average annual growth rate (percentage)
1901	238 396 327	–	–
1911	252 093 390	5.75	0.56
1921	251 321 213	–0.31	–0.03
1931	278 977 238	11.00	1.04
1941	318 660 580	14.22	1.33
1951	361 088 090	13.31	1.25[a]
1961	439 234 771	21.51	1.95[a]
1971	548 159 652	24.80	2.20
1981	683 810 051	24.74	2.22
1991	846 302 688	23.76	2.11

Source: Office of the Registrar General, India.

[a] The growth rates relate to comparable areas.

It is evident from table 1 that the population growth rate was slow up to 1921, owing largely to frequent epidemics of plague and cholera, famine and the influenza epidemic of 1918-1919. Since 1921, there has been an acceleration in the average annual growth rate of the population, which varied between one per cent and one and a half per cent until 1951. The control of various epidemic diseases, improved food security and relief management, and better transport and communication facilities are believed to have contributed to significant reductions in mortality rates and consequent increase in growth rates. Since 1951, there has been further acceleration in population growth rates resulting from faster declines in mortality rates compared with fertility rates. Although the average annual growth rate in 1981-1991 was slightly lower than that for 1971-1981, the current growth rate is still high (figure 2).

Figure 2. Population growth by sex: 1901-1991

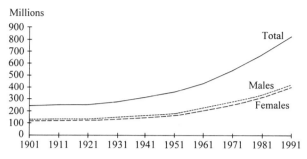

Source: ESCAP, *Socio-economic Profile of SAARC Countries: A Statistical Analysis,* Statistical Profiles No. 1, 1996.

The density of population is estimated to have increased from about 117 per square kilometres in 1951 to about 255 in 1991. The national averages, however, conceal the marked unevenness in population distribution across the country. According to the 1991 census data, West Bengal, which accounts for 8.7 per cent of the total population of the states and only 2.7 per cent of the total area, is the most densely populated state, with 767.1 persons per square kilometre, followed closely by Kerala State (748.7 persons per square kilometre). Bihar (496.8) and Uttar Pradesh (472.5), in the northern Indo-Gangetic Plain, are the third and fourth most densely populated states. The north-eastern areas of India and some states in the northern zone are areas of very low density. The population density of Madhya Pradesh, Rajasthan, Karnataka, Orissa and Andhra Pradesh is below the national average (table 2).

The population is predominantly rural, with about 74 per cent of the total residing in approximately 600,000 villages. Even though India is among the less urbanized countries in the region, the number of Indians living in urban areas is phenomenal. The country's urban population increased more than eightfold from

Table 2. Population distribution and density by state: 1991 census

State	Area		1991 population		Population density, 1991 (per square kilometre)
	Square kilometre	Percent-age	Number	Percent-age	
Andhra Pradesh	275 068	8.4	66 508 008	8.0	241.8
Arunachal Pradesh	83 743	2.6	864 558	0.1	10.3
Assam	78 438	2.4	22 414 322	2.7	285.8
Bihar	173 877	5.3	86 374 465	10.3	469.8
Goa	3 702	0.1	1 169 793	0.1	316.0
Gujarat	196 024	6.0	41 309 582	4.9	210.7
Haryana	44 212	1.3	16 463 648	2.0	372.4
Himachal Pradesh	55 673	1.7	5 170 877	0.6	92.9
Jammu and Kashmir	222 236	6.8	7 718 700	0.9	34.7
Karnataka	191 791	5.9	44 977 201	5.4	234.5
Kerala	38 863	1.2	29 098 518	3.5	748.7
Madhya Pradesh	443 446	13.5	66 181 170	7.9	149.2
Maharashtra	307 690	9.4	78 937 187	9.5	256.5
Manipur	22 327	0.7	1 837 149	0.2	82.3
Meghalaya	22 429	0.7	1 774 778	0.2	79.1
Mizoram	21 081	0.6	689 756	0.1	32.7
Nagaland	16 579	0.5	1 209 546	0.1	73.0
Orissa	155 707	4.8	31 659 736	3.8	203.3
Punjab	50 362	1.5	20 281 969	2.4	402.7
Rajasthan	342 239	10.4	44 005 990	5.3	128.6
Sikkim	7 096	0.2	406 457	0.1	57.3
Tamil Nadu	130 058	4.0	55 858 946	6.7	429.4
Tripura	10 486	0.3	2 757 205	0.3	262.9
Uttar Pradesh	294 411	9.0	139 112 287	16.7	472.5
West Bengal	88 752	2.7	68 077 965	8.2	767.1
All states	3 276 290	100.0	834 859 813	100.0	254.8

Source: ESCAP, *Socio-Economic Profile of SAARC Countries: A Statistical Analysis,* Statistical Profiles No. 1, 1996.

a mere 25.9 million in 1901 to 217.6 million in 1991. During this period, the proportion of the total population living in urban areas increased from 10.8 to 25.7 per cent. The decadal growth of the urban population had increased very significantly after 1931, reaching a high of 46.1 per cent during the period 1971-1981; there was a slowing down in this growth during the period 1981-1991 (table 3 and figure 3).

The increase in urban population has also been occasioned by an increase in the number of urban agglomerations/towns, from 1,827 in 1901 to 3,768 in 1991. An important feature of India's urbanization is the increasing concentration of people in large towns and cities, that is, those with a population of 100,000 or more. In 1991, of the 3,768 urban agglomerations, 300 had a population exceeding 100,000 each and these 300 areas together accounted for nearly two thirds of all urban residents. The four largest metropolitan cities, Mumbai (Bombay), Calcutta, Delhi and Madras, had a combined population of 25.4 million. During the past two decades, cities such as Bangalore, Ahmedabad and Hyderabad have expanded rapidly as new industrial cities. The growth of most urban centres have largely been due to internal expansion rather than rural-to-urban migration.

4. Ethnicity

India is heterogeneous with respect to ethnic origins, languages and religion, and for this reason has often been referred to as an "ethnological museum". There are about 225

languages spoken in the country, although only 15 of them are considered major languages. By and large, these languages belong to two great language families: Indo-Aryan and Dravidian. The former, spoken by over 71 per cent of the people and mostly residing in the north, include Hindi, Rajasthani, Bihari, Bengali, Oriya and Marathi. The four languages spoken in south India, Tamil, Malayalam, Kannada and Telugu, belong to the Dravidian group. There are also many tribal languages spoken in the jungle areas and the Tibetan languages in the Himalayas. An interesting demographic feature of India is the concentration of the different linguistic groups in specific states; indeed, language forms the main basis of the division of the federal Union into states. Hindi, which is widely spoken, particularly in the north, is the official language of the Union. English is also spoken and understood by many educated people.

Figure 3. Growth of urban and rural population: 1901-1981

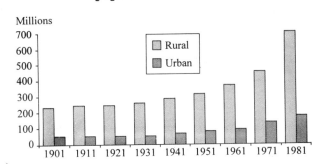

Source: ESCAP, *Socio-economic Profile of SAARC Countries: A Statistical Analysis*, Statistical Profiles No. 1, 1996.

Table 3. Trend of urbanization: 1901-1911

Census year	Number of urban agglomerations	Urban population	Urban as percentage of total population	Percentage decadal growth
1901	1 827	25 851 873	10.84	–
1911	1 815	25 941 633	10.29	0.35
1921	1 949	28 086 167	11.18	8.27
1931	2 072	33 455 989	11.99	19.12
1941	2 250	44 153 297	13.86	31.97
1951	2 843	62 443 709	17.29	41.42
1961	2 365	78 936 603	17.97	26.41
1971	2 590	109 113 977	19.91	38.23
1981	2 378	159 462 547	23.34	46.14
1991	2 768	217 611 012	25.71	36.46

Source: Office of the Registrar General, India, *Census of India, 1991, Series 1*, Paper No. 2 of 1992.

Hinduism is the most important religion in India, in that over 80 per cent of the people are adherents of one or the other of the Hindu sects. In 1991, about 102 million Indians were reported to be Muslims, making India one of the largest Muslim-populated countries in the world. In addition, there were about 20 million Christians, 16 million Sikhs, 6 million Buddhists and 3 million Jains. India is also home to one of the world's few remaining communities of Parsis, adherents of the faith of Zoroastrianism.

Indian society is also characterized by a large number of caste groups, each of which is endogamous and into one of which a person enters irrevocably at birth. The caste hierarchy provides the framework for determining one's status and to some extent one's occupation. However, the disadvantaged groups are provided special support and safeguards under the Constitution, which contains a schedule of the castes and tribes eligible to receive special benefits, including welfare services, scholarships, and guaranteed places in educational institutions, the civil service and Parliament. Further, with increased education and helped by the anonymity of the urban environment, caste distinctions are becoming less acute, with little relevance for daily social interactions. The scheduled castes account for about 15-16 per cent and the scheduled tribes 7-8 per cent of the national population.

5. The economy

The Indian economy is the world's sixth biggest in terms of purchasing power parity and is also arguably one of the most industrialized in the world, with a high level of indigenous technological achievements covering areas such as nuclear energy, space and satellite communications, oceanography, deep-sea oil drilling, and armaments manufacture. Yet, India is one of the poorest countries in the world, with a per capita gross national product (GNP) estimated at US$ 331 in 1992.

Despite such a lowly status, India has recorded impressive improvements in GDP growth, from an average of 3.5 per cent during the 1960s and early 1970s to 5.0 per cent in 1975-1984 and further to 5.9 per cent in 1985-1995. The acceleration in growth rates during the 1980s was partly due to the spread of the "green revolution" and partly to an acceleration in the rate of industrial expansion. The growth experience of the 1980s, however, was not sustained in the early 1990s, when the GDP growth rate declined to an average of 3.6 per cent during the period 1990-1992 owing to the slow-down occasioned by stabilization and structural adjustments in the wake of the 1991 crisis. Thereafter there was a rapid recovery and the growth rate increased to 5 per cent in 1993, 6.3 per cent in 1994/95 and further to 7.0 per cent in 1995/96. The acceleration in growth rates in recent years has largely been attributed to the fruits of an array of reforms and the deepening of the reform efforts in some areas, and the identification of new priorities for policy action.

The pattern of GDP growth that has taken place during the past four decades inevitably led to a shift in the sectoral composition of output. The share of the agricultural sector in GDP had declined from about 55 per cent in the early 1950s to about 33 per cent in the late 1980s. Concomitantly, there has been an increase in the relative contribution of manufacturing, from about 12 to 20 per cent, and also of the tertiary sectors (table 4). Despite its diminishing share in total GDP, the agricultural sector continues to play a crucial role in the Indian economy, contributing an estimated 32 per cent of GDP in 1993/94 and absorbing an overwhelmingly large proportion (70 per cent) of the total labour force.

By and large, India has achieved remarkable progress in industrial and agricultural production. Food grains production, both cereals and pulses, has risen owing to improved agricultural practices resulting in higher productivity per hectare. For instance, the net production of cereals increased from 40 million tonnes in 1950/51 to 191 million tonnes in 1994. The per capita per day availability of cereals and pulses has also increased over the years, while the production of milk, eggs and fish has risen significantly.

Despite overall economic growth, a substantial proportion of the country's population

Table 4. Sectoral distribution of gross domestic product

(Percentage share)

Sector	1951/52 to 1955/56	1956/57 to 1960/61	1961/62 to 1965/66	1966/67 to 1970/71	1971/72 to 1975/76	1976/77 to 1980/81	1981/82 to 1985/86	1985/86 to 1989/90	1992/93
Agriculture	54.91	51.86	46.61	43.76	42.04	38.75	36.48	32.82	31.82
Mining and quarrying	1.15	1.18	1.39	1.45	1.38	1.46	1.69	1.76	2.24
Manufacturing	11.88	13.47	15.77	16.17	16.95	18.02	18.85	20.00	17.48
Electricity, gas and water	0.38	0.53	0.79	1.11	1.33	1.62	1.84	2.14	2.18
Construction	3.37	3.89	4.56	5.32	4.74	4.91	4.64	4.43	5.53
Trade, hotels, restaurants	8.62	9.38	10.46	10.82	11.05	11.89	12.21	12.67	12.68
Transport, storage, communications	2.51	2.84	3.23	3.53	3.90	4.42	4.77	5.26	7.92
Financing etc.	8.88	8.56	8.29	8.20	8.45	8.83	9.02	9.84	8.18
Public administration and defence	2.24	2.48	3.05	3.63	4.17	4.42	4.84	5.48	5.73
Other services	6.07	5.82	5.84	6.01	5.98	5.69	5.65	5.60	6.23
Total	100.00	100.0	100.00	100.00	100.00	100.00	100.00	100.00	100.00

Source: Planning Commission, Delhi, *Eighth Five-year Plan (1992-1997),* vol. I.

continues to live in a state of dire poverty. Although the incidence of poverty is estimated to have declined significantly over the years, the 1993/94 official estimates place the population below the poverty line at 169 million, or 19 per cent of the total population. These estimates also indicate that the incidence of poverty is concentrated in the rural areas; in 1993/94, more than a fifth of the rural people were living in poverty, compared with only a little over one tenth in the urban areas (table 5). The majority of the rural poor are landless labourers, small and marginal farmers, fishermen, rural artisans and people belonging to backward castes and tribes. Generally, the rural poor have either no assets or assets with low productivity, few relevant skills, and either have no regular full-time jobs or are employed in very low-paid jobs; there is also a large degree of inter-state variation in the incidence of poverty, the proportion below the poverty line ranging from a low of 10 per cent in Haryana and Punjab to 35 per cent in Uttar Pradesh, Madhya Pradesh and Bihar and further to 45 per cent in Orissa.

According to a 1989/90 survey, an important change appears to be the emergence of a large middle class with incomes adequate to command a life style with an expanding range of consumer goods. The survey data revealed

Table 5. Estimates of poverty incidence: 1972/73 to 1987/88

Year	Poverty incidence (percentage)		
	All India	Urban	Rural
1972/73	51.5	41.2	54.1
1977/78	48.3	38.2	51.2
1983/84	37.4	28.1	40.1
1987/88	29.4	20.1	33.4
1993/94	19.0	11.6	21.7

Source: Economic Survey, 1993/94 and *1995/96.*

that of the 142 million households in the country, 58.6 million, or approximately 41 per cent, were in receipt of annual incomes exceeding Rs 12,500, which was sufficient to command a life style which included a growing range of consumer goods, and that this proportion was much higher (62.8 per cent) in urban than in rural (32.7 per cent) areas.

6. Social infrastructure

(a) Education

In India, the systematic development of education started only after the country achieved independence in 1947, and in particular with the enactment of the Constitution of India in 1950 and the initiation of country-wide social planning in 1952. The Constitution provides the basic framework for educational development in the country and the relevant articles mandate the Union government and the government of each state and territory to provide free and compulsory education for all children until they complete the age of 14 years. The Constitution has also made it obligatory for state and Union governments to provide scholarships and stipends, in addition to free education, to scheduled castes and scheduled tribes and students from backward communities.

There are some variations in the structure of school education between the states. The primary stage consists of the first five years of schooling comprising classes/grades I-V in some states, and the first four years of schooling (grades I-IV) in others. The middle stage includes three years of schooling after the primary stage and comprises grades V-VII or VI-VIII, depending on the pattern of classes prevalent in the state or territory. The primary and middle stages together constitute the elementary stage, which would normally comprise grades I-VII or I-VIII.

In most cases, grades IX-X constitute the secondary stage, and schools having this pattern are referred to as "high schools". In some states, the secondary stage terminates only at the end of grade XI, and schools adopting this pattern are referred to as higher secondary schools. In some states and union territories where the secondary stage terminates at the end of grade X, there exists a stage of school education called the higher/senior secondary stage, comprising grades XI-XII. However, in the case of a few states, the higher senior secondary stage forms part of the college education, often referred to as the intermediate or pre-degree stage.

It should, however, be noted that following the recommendations of the 1964-1966 Education Commission, practically all states and union territories are gradually adopting the 10 + 2 pattern of school education, comprising primary, middle, secondary and higher levels. By and large, grades I-V constitute the primary cycle, grades VI-VIII the middle stage, grades IX-X the secondary level, and grades XI-XII

the higher secondary stage. A child is normally admitted to grade I at the age of 6 and is expected to complete grade V at the age of about 11 years, and grade VIII at the age of about 14 years. Thus, grades I-VIII are deemed to constitute the elementary stage of school education for children aged 6-14 years, and it is in respect of this age group that efforts are being made to universalize education.

Since 1950, India has achieved remarkable progress in providing educational facilities and opportunities in all states and union territories, and this progress is reflected in the phenomenal increase in the number of educational institutions and of teachers and students. Table 6 shows the number of schools, teachers and students in the country in 1992/93.

Table 6. Number of schools, teachers and students: 1992/93

Educational level	Schools	Teachers	Students
Primary	572 541	1 681 970	105 370 216
Middle	153 921	1 082 345	38 708 581
Secondary (High school)	62 984	837 871	15 753 586
Higher secondary (New pattern)	18 888	515 077	4 793 091

Source: Planning, Monitoring and Statistics Division, Department of Education, Ministry of Human Resources Development.

Available data also indicate that the gross enrolment ratio had increased from 42.6 per cent in 1950/51 to 105.7 per cent in 1992/93 at the primary level (class I-V) and from 12.7 to 67.5 per cent in the upper primary stage (class VI-VIII) during the same period. The proportion of children moving from the primary to upper primary stages had also increased steadily, from 16.3 per cent in 1950/51 to about 34 per cent in 1991/92. The overall literacy rate had also almost trebled, from 18.3 per cent in 1951 to 52.2 per cent in 1991.

Despite the progress made, there are still marked disparities in educational participation and educational attainment between various states and union territories, between urban and rural areas, and between males and females.

These aspects will be discussed in detail in the next section of this profile. However, it may be noted that the basic objectives of the government's Eighth Five-year Plan (1992-1997) are universalization of elementary education and eradication of illiteracy in the age group 15-35 years.

(b) Health

The present health-oriented developmental activities in India have their origin in the recommendations of the Health Survey and Development Committee (popularly known as the Bhore Committee) set up in 1943. The proposals of this Committee for the future development of the country's health sector were based on the following five main principles:

(a) That no individual should fail to secure adequate medical care because of the inability the pay for it;

(b) The health programme must, from the very beginning, lay special emphasis on preventive work with consequential development of environmental hygiene;

(c) The health services should be placed as close to the people as possible in order to ensure the maximum benefit to the communities to be served;

(d) It is essential to secure the active cooperation of the people in the development of health programmes, and the active support of the people is to be sought through the establishment of a Health Committee in every village;

(e) The doctor who is the leader of the health team should be a "social physician" who should combine remedial and preventive measures so as to confer the maximum benefit on the community.

Starting from the First Five-year Plan, the basic public health strategy consisted of expansion of the physical infrastructure, including mother-and-child health (MCH) centres, family planning programme, control of communicable diseases, and expansion and training of health personnel, especially women workers, including trained birth attendants. In 1983, the Government of India adopted a National Health Policy in the context of the worldwide objective of "Health for All by the Year 2000". The primary health care approach adopted by the government has enabled health facilities and services to be easily accessible to an increasing proportion of the population, particularly in the rural areas.

Over the years, India has made considerable progress in enhancing the health status of its population. Health facilities and personnel have increased tremendously during the past four decades (table 7). Apart from the government health system, there is a large number of privately organized hospitals, health centres and dispensaries, some of which extend concessional medical care to the economically weaker

Table 7. Number of health institutions, facilities and health personnel: 1951-1992

Type of health institutions/ facilities/personnel	1951	1961	1971	1981	1991	1992
Medical colleges	28	60	98	111	128	146
Hospitals	2 694	3 094	3 862	6 804	11 174	13 692
Dispensaries	6 515	9 406	12 180	16 751	27 431	27 403
Community health centres	–	–	–	217	2 071	2 193
Primary health centres	725	2 565	5 112	5 740	20 450	20 719
Subcentres	–	–	28 489	51 405	130 958	131 454
Hospital beds (all types)	117 178	230 000	348 655	569 495	810 548	n.a.
Doctors	61 840	83 756	151 129	268 712	394 068	410 875
Dentists	3 290	3 582	5 512	8 648	10 751	11 300
Nurses	16 550	35 584	80 620	154 280	340 208	385 410

Source: Government of India, *Economic Survey, 1995/96.*

n.a. = not available.

sections. In addition, a large number of indigenous medical practitioners serve the vast majority of the rural population.

During the past four decades, there have been very significant declines in the incidence of morbidity and mortality in the country. Smallpox has been eradicated and plague is no longer a problem; the incidence of malaria had declined sharply during the post-independence period and is now under surveillance, while morbidity due to cholera etc. has declined considerably. Consequently, the crude death rate is estimated to have declined from about 27 per thousand in 1951 to about 10 per thousand in 1992, while life expectancy at birth increased from 32.1 to 60.3 years during the same period.

Despite these improvements, health standards in the country are generally poor, although the number of trained doctors is relatively large. Communicable diseases still account for more than two thirds of total morbidity and mortality nationwide. The infant mortality rate remained at an unacceptably high level of 82 in 1992. The vast majority of the population lack access to adequate sanitation facilities; only about 2 per cent of the rural population has access to such facilities. A significant feature of the health system appears to be its maldistribution, biased in favour of urban upper and middle classes and against the rural poor.

(c) Water supply and sanitation

Significant strides have been made in India in regard to the supply of safe drinking water to the country's population, especially in the underserved villages. The proportion of the rural population with access to safe drinking water increased from 56.3 per cent in 1985 to 82.8 per cent in 1995, and from 72.9 to 84.9 per cent in respect of the urban population during the same period (table 8), mainly as a result of the efforts made during the International Drinking Water Supply and Sanitation Decade (1981-1991).

As noted earlier, sanitation is one of the weakest links of development in both rural and urban areas and progress in extending sani-

Table 8. Percentage of population covered by drinking water and sanitation facilities, by urban/rural area: 1985-1995

Facility and residence	1985	1990	1995
Drinking water supply			
Urban	72.9	83.8	84.9
Rural	56.3	73.9	82.8
Sanitation facilities			
Urban	28.4	45.9	47.9
Rural	0.7	2.4	3.6

Source: Government of India, *Economic Survey, 1995/96.*

tary facilities has remained extremely slow. Sanitary means of excreta disposal are practically non-existent in rural areas, while more than half the urban population do without them (table 8). Hence, the Government's Eighth Five-year Plan (1992-1997) lays emphasis on a Total Environmental Sanitation approach in rural areas making information, education and communication (IEC) an integral part of the programme, and on the elimination of manual scavenging.

7. Development planning

India has opted to charter its development through five-year plans which lay down the development goals and strategies, identify the main policy instruments and programmes (including those relating to women's development) and determine outlays for various development sectors. The formulation, financing and implementation of the five-year plans constitute a joint endeavour of the central and state/union territory governments. The relative contributions of these governments to various developmental activities in the Eighth Five-year Plan are shown in annex table B.1. It will be noted that allocation for social services constitutes 18.20 per cent of the total public sector outlay in the current Plan; this proportion is significantly higher than the 14.56 per cent of the total allocated in the Sixth Plan (1980-1985) and the 15.98 per cent allocated in the Seventh Plan (1985-1990).

Allocations for various components of the social services programme in the Eighth Plan are shown in annex table B.2. It will be noted that within the social services sector, the largest shares are for education, health and family welfare, and water supply and sanitation.

The Eighth Plan represents a departure from the earlier planning strategies. It is indicative in nature and attempts to dovetail planning needs and the market mechanisms so that they function in a complementary manner. The plan strategy seeks to free the economy from unnecessary controls and regulations and introduce reforms to provide greater stimulus to the private sector in industrial development. The Plan also lays emphasis on redirecting the development process and reshaping strategies towards reducing the human problems of mass unemployment, poverty and inequality. Among other things, the Plan attempts to provide constructive opportunities for women to express their talents and energies so as to enable them to lead a life of dignity and security.

C. WOMEN'S PROFILE

1. Demographic characteristics

(a) Sex composition

In India, as in many other countries of the region, males outnumber females in the total population. The excess of males (or deficit of females) is not an accident of any one census but has been a demographic phenomenon highlighted by all decennial censuses carried out in the country (table 9).

It will be noted from table 9 that the proportionate share of females in the total population had gradually declined, from 49.2 per cent in 1901 to 48.1 per cent in 1991. Consequently, the number of males per 100 females had increased fairly steadily from 102.9 to 107.9, while the number of females per 100 males decreased from 97.2 to 92.7 during the same period.

The deficit of females in the total population has usually been attributed to the interplay of several factors, such as greater underenumeration of females at the censuses, a male-favoured sex ratio at birth, and higher female than male mortality.

(i) Under-enumeration of females

In view of the greater inaccuracies in the age returns for females and taking into consideration the socio-cultural attitudes towards females prevalent in various parts of the country, it was often argued that the observed imbalance between the number of males and females in the general population was largely due to the under-enumeration of females at the censuses. At the time of the 1881 census, for instance, it was observed that "the main cause of the apparent disparity is the omission to give

Table 9. Population classified by sex, percentage of females and sex ratios: censuses of 1901 to 1991

Census year	Enumerated population			Percent-age female	Males per 100 females	Females per 100 males
	Both sexes	Male	Female			
1901	238 396 327[a/]	120 791 301	117 358 672	49.23	102.92	97.16
1911	252 093 390	128 385 368	123 708 022	49.07	103.78	96.36
1921	251 321 213	128 546 225	122 774 988	48.85	104.70	95.51
1931	278 977 238[a/]	142 929 689	135 788 921	48.67	105.26	95.00
1941	318 660 580[a/]	163 685 302	154 690 267	48.54	105.81	94.50
1951	361 088 090	185 528 462	175 559 628	48.62	105.68	94.63
1961	439 234 771	226 293 201	212 941 570	48.48	106.27	94.10
1971	548 159 652	284 049 276	264 110 376	48.18	107.54	92.98
1981	683 810 051	353 347 249	330 462 802	48.33	106.92	93.52
1991	846 302 688	439 230 458	407 072 230	48.10	107.90	92.68

Source: Office of the Registrar General, India, Census of India, 1981: General Population Tables; and Census of India, 1991, Paper No. 2 of 1992.

[a/] A classification of the population of Pondicherry by sex for 1901 (246, 354), 1931 (258, 628) and 1941 (285, 011) is not available. The figures in respect of India for these years are, therefore, exclusive of these population figures so far as distribution by sex is concerned.

correct count of the females". However, it was not until the 1951 census that attempts were made to ascertain the extent of under-enumeration of males as well as females. The post-enumeration check that was carried out to verify the degree of under-enumeration in respect of the 1951 census revealed that a larger proportion of females than males were omitted in the census count in all parts of the country except Central India. This finding was also confirmed by the post-enumeration checks carried out in respect of the 1961 census. The extent of under-enumeration at the 1971 census was provisionally estimated at 2.15 per cent for males and 2.50 per cent for females.

While a relatively greater under-count of females might have been prevalent in the past censuses, there is no evidence to suggest that the quality of the census count has deteriorated in recent decades, particularly as regards the enumeration of females. On the other hand, the custom of purdah, which was earlier considered to be responsible for the under-reporting of females, has been gradually vanishing in various parts of the country with the increasing participation of women in education and employment, and hence one would expect a reduction in female under-enumeration and not an increase to warrant the observed rise in the sex ratio (males per 100 females) over the years.

(ii) Sex ratio at birth

Data from a wide variety of countries around the world show conclusively that the sex ratio at birth favours males, with 104-106 male births per 100 female births every year. In India, it is not possible to obtain accurate estimates of the sex ratio at birth for the country as well as the constituent states and union territories owing to the inherent defects in the vital registration system, as well as the substantial under-reporting of events. However, the sex ratios at birth during the 1950s and 1960s as reported by the registration system are given in annex table C.1.

It will be noted from annex table C.1 that the average sex ratio at birth for Group A states, or states where registration data are considered to be more reliable, was 112.4 in

1966, and that this ratio shows an increase from 109.9 in 1956. Even within the Group A states, the 1966 ratio had varied from a low of 104.2 in Kerala to 123.5 in Uttar Pradesh. Within the Group B states and union territories which were considered to have had less reliable data, the reported sex ratio in 1966 was usually high in most areas.

In order to obtain more reliable estimates of births and deaths, a sample registration system was started in some areas in 1964 and has been gradually extended to cover all states and union territories. According to the full-scale study conducted in four states, Gujarat, Kerala, Maharashtra and Mysore (present Karnataka), the sex ratio at birth in 1965-1967 ranged from a low of 105.3 in Kerala to a high of 111.1 in Mysore. Data from the Sample Registration System for recent years also give a very high sex ratio at birth (110.1 for 1989-1991); these data also show that the sex ratio at birth for the country as a whole had increased from 108.9 in 1981-1983 to 110.1 in 1989-1991 (table 10).

Table 10. Sex ratios at birth: 1981-1991

Period	Sex ratio at birth (males/100 females)
1981-1983	108.9
1982-1984	109.8
1983-1985	110.4
1984-1986	109.6
1985-1987	109.6
1986-1988	109.7
1987-1989	109.9
1988-1990	109.7
1989-1991	110.1

Source: Office of the Registrar General, India, as reported in Central Statistical Organization, *Women and Men in India, 1995* (New Delhi, Ministry of Planning, Government of India, 1995).

Note: Figures are based on the data from the *Sample Registration System.*

Although the data from the statutory registration system as well as the Sample Registration System yield estimates of sex ratios at birth which are unusually high by global norms, a 1964 analysis based on over 1.9 million births that took place in hospitals and health centres throughout India during the period 1949-1958 estimated the sex ratio at birth at 106.4 male births per 100 female births for the country as a whole, with a slight variation from 103.9 for the northern zone to 108.2 for the central zone (table 11). The sex ratio at birth as reported by the 1964 analysis could be considered to be more accurate and realistic as the analysis was based on more reliable data, and the estimate is in accordance with estimates for many other countries in the world.

(iii) Sex-differential mortality

On account of the defectiveness of the vital registration system and under-reporting of vital events, it is not possible to obtain reliable direct estimates of mortality rates for both males and females in India. Nevertheless, various indirect estimates suggest that for a long time in the past, the incidence of morbidity as well as mortality has been higher among females than among males. In particular, females continue to be exposed to greater risks of death at childhood (between the age of one month and four years) and at peak childbearing ages, 15-35 years. The gender disparity in mortality or survival has been attributed to several factors which are in one way or other connected to the traditional socio-cultural preference for sons and in-built prejudice and discrimination against women.

Studies carried out in various parts of India have shown conclusively that gender is by and large a significant determinant of the nutritional and health status of the population. Indian women have less access to health services and facilities than their male counterparts. For every three men who avail themselves of health services, only one woman does so, because clinics are often not open at times that are convenient for women and generally a woman seems not to seek treatment unless she is severely ill. Second, while the nutritional status of the generality of men, women and children is low, that of women seems to be even lower. The caloric and micro-nutrient intake is relatively less among girls than boys (table 12).

The gender differential in regard to food and nutrition intakes starts at infancy, when girls are not only weaned earlier than boys but are also not provided with adequate supplementary nutrition. For example, a 1984 study reported that in the southern state of Tamil Nadu, male children were breastfed on an average for five months longer than female children, and that male children in land-owning families were breastfed almost 10 months longer than female children in agricultural labourer households. Several studies conducted in the 1970s and 1980s have also reported that generally girls receive lower-quality health care than boys.

The neglect of female children in regard to food, nutrition and health care has resulted in mortality rates of children aged 0-4 years being higher for female than for male children. For instance, according to the data

Table 11. Sex ratios at birth based on live births recorded in hospitals and health centres by zone: 1949-1958

Zone	Number of reporting health institutions	Number of live births		Sex ratio at birth (males/100 females)
		Male	Female	
India	549	995 601	935 626	106.4
North	16	51 557	49 615	103.9
East	28	254 523	241 099	105.6
South	358	379 558	356 658	106.4
West	52	146 185	136 142	107.4
Central	24	50 483	46 653	108.2
North-west	71	113 295	105 459	107.4

Source: K.V. Ramachandran and Vinayak A. Deshpande, "The sex ratio at birth in India by regions" in *The Milbank Memorial Fund Quarterly*, vol. 42, No. 2 (Part I), 1964.

Table 12. Daily average intake of energy and protein by age group and sex: 1990

Age group	Energy (calories/day)		Protein (grams/day)	
	Male	Female	Male	Female
1-3	780	773	22.0	21.9
4-6	1 112	1 097	31.5	30.9
7-9	1 325	1 320	39.0	36.0
10-12	1 550	1 483	42.9	41.0
13-15	1 773	1 620	49.1	42.9
16-18	1 937	1 721	58.6	47.7
>18	2 169	1 789	62.0	50.4

Source: National Institute of Nutrition, Hyderabad, reported in Central Statistical Organization, *Women and Men in India, 1995* (New Delhi, Ministry of Planning, Government of India, 1995).

from the Office of the Registrar General, the 1987 mortality rate for female children (36.8 per cent) was 3.2 percentage points higher than the rate of 33.6 per cent reported for their male counterparts (table 13). Available data also indicate that females have been experiencing higher mortality rates than men during adolescence and early adulthood (annex table C.2) owing to the "triple burden" of reproduction, household chores and productive work, in addition to relatively poor nutrition and health care.

In most human populations, the initial advantage of excess male births tends to be reduced or even eliminated by higher infant mortality rates for males. But in India, the higher mortality among female infants and children has helped to perpetuate the imbalance in the sex proportions occurring at birth, and until recently the higher female mortality at practically all subsequent ages appears to have

greatly enhanced the balance in favour of males throughout life. However, it is difficult to explain why the early part of this century, when factors related to the mortality of women were far more adverse, shows a more even sex ratio. Further, the gender gap in mortality rates has been narrowing over the years and in recent years the crude death rate of females has been lower and life expectancy higher than that of males, and yet the sex ratio, or number of males per 100 females in the total population, has been reported to be increasing.

The adverse sex ratio is a matter of great concern and is often cited as an indication of women's low status. In the absence of convincing evidence, it is difficult to ascertain the extent to which factors such as sex ratio at birth, under-enumeration of females, differences in rate of decline of mortality for males and females, migration, prenatal sex determination leading to aborting of the female foetus and

Table 13. Death rates for children aged 0-4 years by residence and sex: 1970-1987

Year	India			Urban			Rural		
	Both sexes	Male	Female	Both sexes	Male	Female	Both sexes	Male	Female
1970	53.0	51.7	55.1	32.3	32.3	32.3	57.8	55.5	61.0
1978	50.1	50.0	50.2	30.7	30.0	31.1	54.1	54.0	54.3
1984	41.2	39.5	43.0	23.2	22.6	23.8	46.2	44.2	48.2
1985	38.4	36.6	40.4	20.7	19.4	22.1	43.3	41.4	45.3
1986	36.6	34.7	38.6	20.9	20.3	21.5	40.8	38.6	43.3
1987	35.2	33.6	36.8	18.2	18.1	18.5	39.7	37.8	41.8

Source: Office of the Registrar General, India, reported in UNICEF, *Children and Women in India: A Situation Analysis, 1990* (New Delhi, 1991).

other factors play a role in the reported increase in the sex ratio of the general population. Further careful investigation of these factors is needed to enable appropriate measures to be taken to reverse the trend. In this connection, it may be noted that Maharashtra State has banned prenatal tests for determining the sex of the foetus, and that in July 1994, the Lok Sabha passed a bill banning the use of prenatal diagnostic techniques for determining the sex of a baby.

(iv) Differential sex ratios

While the number of females is lower than the number of males in the country, this deficit appears to be more marked in urban than in rural areas. The number of females per 1,000 males declined steadily between 1901 and 1991 in both the urban and rural areas, and in 1991, this ratio was 938 in rural compared with 894 in urban areas (table 14). The larger deficit of females or the greater excess of males among the urban population has largely to be attributed to a predominance of males in the rural-to-urban migration streams.

Table 14. Sex ratios in India and urban and rural areas: 1901-1991

Year	Sex ratio (females per 1,000 males)		
	India	Urban	Rural
1901	972	910	979
1911	964	872	975
1921	955	846	970
1931	950	838	966
1941	945	831	965
1951	946	860	965
1961	941	845	963
1971	930	858	949
1981[a/]	934	879	951
1991[b/]	927	894	938

Source: Office of the Registrar General, India.

[a/] Excluding Assam.
[b/] Excluding Jammu and Kashmir.

There is also large variation in the sex composition of the population among the states and union territories. In 1981, only Kerala State had an excess of females, but all other states and union territories had a deficit of females. The number of females per 1,000 males ranged from a low of 760 in Andaman and Nicoban Island and 769 in Chandigarh to 868 in Delhi, 835 in Sikkim, 862 in Arunachal Pradesh to 977 in Tamil Nadu and 1,032 in Kerala (annex table C.3).

(b) Age structure

The decline in fertility and mortality has resulted in significant changes in the age structure of the Indian population over the years, as is evident from the percentage distribution of the population by five-year age groups and sex for selected years from 1970 to 1992 given in annex table C.4. It will be noted that during this 22-year period, the percentage share of young persons has been declining, with concomitant increases in the relative shares of persons in old-age groups and in working ages.

The percentage distribution of the population by broad age groups 0-14, corresponding to dependent children, 60 and above, representing the elderly, and 15-59, encompassing persons in working ages, is shown in table 15 (see also figure 4).

It will be noted from table 15 that the proportion of children (0-14 years) in the total population had declined steadily, from about 42 per cent in 1970 to about 36 per cent in 1992, owing to the decline in overall fertility rates during this period. It will also be noted that the proportionate share of children in the total population has always been slightly lower among females compared with males; in 1992, female children constituted 35.8 per cent of all females, the corresponding proportion among males being 36.3 per cent. The proportion of elderly persons (60 +) has always been slightly high among females owing to the higher survival rates for females compared with males at these ages. These proportions for both males and females have been rising gradually over the years and in 1992, the elderly constituted 6.5 per cent among all females compared with 5.8 per cent among males. The relative share of persons in working ages 15-59 increased steadily for both males and females, from about 53.0 per cent in 1970 to 58 per cent in 1992.

Table 15. Percentage distribution of population by broad age group and sex, and dependency ratios: 1970-1992

Age group	1970		1980		1990		1992	
	Male	Female	Male	Female	Male	Female	Male	Female
0-14	41.7	41.6	38.2	37.8	37.1	36.5	36.3	35.8
15-59	53.0	52.8	56.2	56.2	57.2	57.0	57.9	57.7
60+	5.3	5.6	5.6	6.0	5.7	6.5	5.8	6.5
Dependency ratio[a]	88.7	89.4	77.9	77.9	74.8	75.4	72.7	73.3

Source: Office of the Registrar General, India, *Sample Registration System.*

[a] Referring to number of persons aged 0-14 years and 60 years and over per 100 persons aged 15-59 years.

Figure 4. Age-sex pyramid of India: 1995

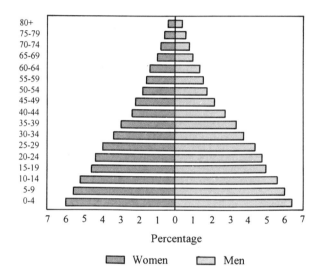

Source: United Nations, *Sex and Age Distribution of the World Population: The 1994 Revision.*

Despite the changes in the age structure that had taken place over the years, India's population is still young in the sense that children and youth together constituted 46.0 per cent among all females and 47.2 per cent among males in 1992 (annex table C.4). This youthful age structure has both demographic and economic implications. Demographically, a young age structure has built-in potential for a further substantial increase in the country's population because annually the number who will be moving into the reproductive ages will be larger than the number who move out of this age group. For example, the number of women in reproductive ages 15-49 as a proportion of all women had increased from 46.7 per cent in 1970 to 50.9 per cent in

1992, thereby resulting in an expansion in the reproductive base over the years, and this trend is likely to continue for the next two decades or so. Thus, given current patterns of family formation, the number of new additions to the population is bound to be substantial, even if there were to be further declines in fertility rates.

The economic implications relate to the high burden of dependency. Children aged 0-14 years and elderly persons aged 60 years and over are usually considered as dependants because generally they do not contribute much to economic productivity and are therefore dependent for their support on persons in the working age. Although the dependency ratios for both males and females has been declining steadily over the years owing to substantial reductions in the proportions of children and increases in the proportions of persons in working ages, in 1992 there were 72.7 males and 73.3 females aged 0-14 years and 60 years and over for every 100 persons aged 15-59 years (table 15). The dependency ratio for females is slightly higher than that for males since the share of women in working ages is lower and the share of elderly women higher than the corresponding proportions for males.

(c) Marital status

Traditionally, the socio-cultural milieu in India had favoured universal and early marriage for women. However, data from the 1961, 1971 and 1981 population censuses show that among persons aged 10 years and over, the proportion reported as never married or single among

23

both males and females has been increasing steadily and significantly since 1961, and that by 1981, about a fourth of rural females and a little less than a third of urban women remained unmarried or single. In all three census years, the proportion never married was higher in urban compared with rural areas and higher among males than females (table 16).

Concurrently with the increase in the proportion never married, there has been a decline in the proportions currently married, widowed and divorced/separated, the three categories which together constitute the ever-married persons. The proportions reported as currently married have always been higher among females than among males and in rural compared with urban areas. In 1981, nearly two thirds of females and about 58 per cent of males aged 10 years and over from rural areas were currently married, compared with 58 per cent of females and 54 per cent of males in urban areas.

It is also evident from table 16 that the proportion reported as widowed was considerably higher among females that among males in both rural and urban areas in all three census years. For example, in 1981 the proportion widowed among females was five times the male proportion in urban areas and thrice the male proportion in rural areas. The considerably higher incidence of widowhood among females is due to a combination of several factors. In the first instance, women in India, as in most other countries of the region, tend to marry men who are five or six years senior to them in age and, given the higher mortality rates at older ages, a larger number of women than men are likely to be widowed every year. Second, under the prevailing social system, a large proportion of widowed males are remarried to single females, while only a small proportion of widowed females are remarried.

The incidence of divorce/separation is very low in India, with less than half of one per cent of men and women reported as being either divorced or separated. Census data also indicate that the incidence of divorce/separation has been declining over the years and that the rate for females is slightly higher than that for males owing to the better chances of remarriage for divorced or separated males compared with their female counterparts.

2. Educational background

(a) Historical scenario

Education, particularly female education, had been a neglected aspect of social development in India for a long time. It was only after

Table 16. Percentage distribution of persons aged 10 years and over by marital status, sex and residence: censuses of 1961, 1971 and 1981

Marital status	Census year	Urban		Rural	
		Male	Female	Male	Female
Never married	1961	39.5	24.1	31.9	15.8
	1971	42.7	29.2	34.7	20.7
	1981	43.8	31.3	37.7	24.0
Currently married	1961	56.4	61.2	61.9	67.5
	1971	54.2	58.9	60.2	65.7
	1981	53.9	58.3	58.2	64.1
Widowed	1961	3.7	14.0	5.6	15.8
	1971	2.6	11.3	4.6	13.0
	1981	2.0	9.9	3.7	11.3
Divorced/separated	1961	0.3	0.6	0.6	0.8
	1971	0.2	0.4	0.4	0.6
	1981	0.2	0.4	0.4	0.6

Source: Office of the Registrar General, India.

the country achieved political independence in 1947 that meaningful steps were initiated towards the systematic development of the education system. The Constitution of India, enacted in 1950, enjoined that "the State shall endeavour to provide, within a period of ten years from the commencement of the Constitution, for free and compulsory education for *all* children until they complete the age of fourteen years". The Constitution also defined "State" to include "the Government and Parliament of India and the government and legislature of each state and all local or other authorities within the territory of India or under the control of the Government of India".

Despite the constitutional mandate and guarantees of non-discrimination on the basis of gender, language, caste etc., the progress in providing elementary education to the increasing population of school-going age, particularly girls, was rather slow in the early years of independence. For example, in 1960/61, only about 41 per cent of the girls aged 6 to 11 years were enrolled in primary classes I-V, the corresponding proportion for boys being 82.6 per cent. Besides lack of adequate access to suitable educational facilities, an important factor responsible for the very low participation of girls in the education system was the societal attitude towards the education of girls, which varied from acceptance of the need to absolute indifference. In the rural areas, particularly among poor families, girls were required to stay at home to perform various domestic chores and to look after the younger siblings, especially if their mothers were engaged in earning a livelihood. Further, the irrelevance of education as then imparted in the schools had adverse effects on parental attitudes towards the education of their daughters.

The government's recognition of the importance of education for girls and of the need for appropriate approaches to increasing their participation in the education system is reflected in various official policy documents, particularly the successive five-year plans. For instance, the First five-year Plan (1950-1955), noting with concern the neglect of women's education, suggested that steps be taken to remove parental prejudices against co-education in primary schools but emphasized the need for setting up separate middle and high schools for girls. The Second Five-year Plan (1955-1960) emphasized, among other things, the need for recruiting and training more women teachers, and providing housing facilities in villages for women teachers as well as incentives for attracting educated married women into the teaching profession.

In 1958, the Government of India set up a National Committee on Women's Education (NCWE) to examine the problems related to the education of girls at primary and secondary levels and to recommend special measures to make up the leeway in women's education at these levels. NCWE recommended, *inter alia,* the creation of special machinery to deal with the problems of education of girls and women at national and subnational levels; provision of adequate finances; and enlisting the professional associations in the promotion of education of girls and women. NCWE also recommended the supply of books, stationery and school uniforms free of charge to girls from poor families, provision of adequate toilet/lavatory facilities, and scholarships to encourage more girls to attend schools. The Committee also recommended that co-education should be adopted as a general principle at the primary stage, and as a transitional measure separate schools should be provided in areas where there was a strong public demand for such facilities and where there was a sufficient number of female students to justify setting up separate schools.

Pursuant to the recommendations of NCWE, the Government of India constituted in 1959 the National Council for Women's Education to advise the Government on issues relating to the education of girls at school level, to suggest policies, programmes and measures for the expansion of girls' education, and to assess the progress achieved from time to time. In 1971, the Government constituted the Committee on the Status of Women in India to examine, among other things, the constitutional, legal and administrative provisions that have a bearing on the social status of women, their education and employment, to consider the development of education among women and to determine the factors responsible for the slow progress. An important recommendation of the Committee was the provision of primary schools within walking distance of the home of every child, and sustained propaganda, preferably by women officials, non-officials, and social and political workers, in order to bring every girl into school.

The recommendations of the various committees are reflected in the government's five-year plans. The Third Five-year Plan (1961-1965) recommended that special emphasis should be laid on creating suitable conditions for encouraging parents to send their daughters to schools, creating public opinion, increasing the number of women from rural areas who would become teachers, and inducing women from urban areas to accept teaching posts in rural areas. Noting the sustained efforts to extend education among girls in primary and middle stages, the Fourth Five-year Plan (1968-1973) recommended that the enrolment of girls should be further increased through the organization of special programmes so as to further reduce the gap in enrolments between boys and girls.

The Sixth Five-year Plan (1980-1985), noting that 100 per cent enrolment of boys had taken place at the primary stage in many parts of the country, recommended the attainment of universalization of girls enrolment up to age 14 within a period of 10 years. For this purpose, the Plan fixed a target of 95 per cent enrolment at the primary stage and 50 per cent enrolment at the middle stage to be achieved by 1984/85, and 100 per cent in respect of both stages to be reached by 1990. The Plan also recommended attaching importance to early education for children aged 3-5 years so that the concept of learning would develop in the children through play and joyful activities, while at the same time freeing their care-takers, usually their elder sisters, to join schools or other educational centres.

(b) Educational participation

(i) Elementary education

Significant progress has been made in regard to the expansion of elementary education over the years of planned development. School enrolment data from the Ministry of Education indicate that between 1950/51 and 1992/93, the number of students enrolled in primary classes I-V had increased more than fivefold from about 19.2 million to 105.4 million, but this increase was more dramatic in regard to girls' enrolments (which increased more than eightfold from 5.4 million to 44.9 million) compared with enrolment of boys (which increased 4.4 times from 13.8 million to 60.4 million). Consequently, the proportion of girls' enrolment to total enrolment at the primary level had increased from 28.1 to 42.6 per cent and the number of girls per 1,000 males enrolled from 391 to 743 during the same 42-year period (table 17 and figure 5).

Table 17. Enrolments at primary and middle school levels by sex, percentage of female enrolment, and females per 1,000 males enrolled: 1950/51 to 1992/93

Year	Primary stage (classes I-V)					Middle stage (classes VI-VIII)				
	Enrolments (thousands)			Percent-age female	Females per 1,000 males	Enrolments (thousands)			Percent-age female	Females per 1,000 males
	Both sexes	Boys	Girls			Both sexes	Boys	Girls		
1950/51	19 155	13 770	5 385	28.1	391	3 120	2 586	534	17.1	206
1960/61	34 994	23 593	11 401	32.6	483	6 705	5 074	1 631	24.3	321
1970/71	57 035	35 729	21 306	37.4	596	13 315	9 426	3 889	29.2	413
1980/81	73 774	45 286	28 488	38.6	629	20 724	13 934	6 790	32.8	487
1990/91	99 119	58 095	41 024	41.4	706	33 283	20 844	12 439	37.4	597
1992/93	105 370	60 454	44 916	42.6	743	38 708	23 693	15 015	38.8	634

Source: Department of Education.

26

Figure 5. Growth of enrolment at primary level by gender: 1950-1951 to 1987-1988

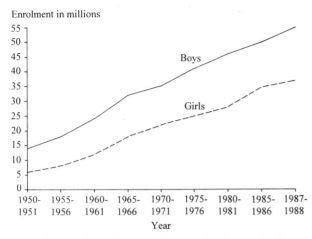

Source: **UNICEF,** *Children and Women in India: A Situation Analysis, 1990* (New Delhi, 1991).

Enrolment trends at the middle or upper primary stage are similar to those at the primary stage, although the numbers involved are much lower, reflecting the slow progress made from the primary to the middle stage level of education. It is clear from table 17 that the total number of pupils enrolled in middle-level classes increased more than twelvefold from 3.1 million in 1950/51 to 38.7 million in 1992/93 and the increase in the enrolment of girls at this level was even more dramatic – a twenty-eightfold increase from 0.53 million to 15.02 million during the same period. Consequently, the proportionate share of girls in total enrolments more than doubled, from 17.1 to 38.8 per cent, while the sex ratio (number of girls per 1,000 boys enrolled) more than trebled, from 206 to 634, during the four decades.

A more appropriate measure of the progress in educational enrolments is the enrolment ratio or the proportion of children enrolled at a particular educational level to the population in relevant ages. It will be noted from table 18 that the gross enrolment ratio for girls increased from 24.6 per cent in 1950/51 to 91.5 per cent in 1994/95 at the primary level and from 4.5 to 52.9 per cent at the middle stage during the same period. It is also evident from table 18 that gross enrolment ratios for girls are substantially lower than for boys at the primary as well as middle stages.

It will be noted from table 18 that the primary-level enrolment ratios had exceeded 100 per cent for boys since 1990/91 and for girls in 1992/93. A ratio exceeding 100 per cent is due to factors such as over-reporting of enrolments (which in most cases is difficult to estimate), and to inclusion in the numerator of under-age and over-age students. Thus, gross enrolment ratios do not give an accurate picture of the enrolment levels or student participation. A more meaningful measure of student participation in the education system is obtained by including in the numerator only those pupils who are of the eligible ages. Estimates of net enrolment rates are not available for India.

Although the proportion of children moving up from the primary to upper primary stage increased steadily from 16.3 per cent in 1950/51 to 34.0 per cent in 1991/92, student participation at the middle or upper primary stage (classes VI-VIII) is relatively low. In 1994/95, the gross enrolment ratio at this level was 77.1

Table 18. Gross enrolment ratios at primary and middle stages by sex: 1950/51 to 1992/93

(Percentage)

Year	Primary stage (classes I-V)			Middle stage (classes VI-VIII)		
	Both sexes	Boys	Girls	Both sexes	Boys	Girls
1950/51	42.6	59.8	24.6	12.7	20.7	4.5
1960/61	62.4	82.6	41.4	22.5	33.2	11.3
1970/71	76.4	92.6	59.1	33.4	46.3	19.9
1980/81	80.5	95.8	64.1	41.9	54.3	28.6
1990/91	101.0	115.3	86.0	60.1	73.4	46.1
1992/93	105.7	118.1	105.7	67.5	80.5	53.8
1994/95	103.0	113.8	91.5	65.5	77.1	52.9

Source: Department of Education.

27

per cent for boys and 53.8 per cent for girls (table 18). Given the limitations of the gross enrolment ratios noted in the preceding paragraph, it could be safely assumed that even in 1994/95 more than a fifth of the boys and over 50 per cent of the girls in the eligible age group were not attending middle-stage classes. Thus, a very substantial proportion of children, particularly girls, aged 6-14 years lack the opportunity to go through the elementary education cycle.

The national average gross enrolment ratios conceal the wide variation in these ratios among the various states. Available data for major states (those with a population of 10 million or more as per the 1991 census) indicate that while the 1994/95 gross enrolment rate for girls at the primary stage exceeds 100 per cent in six states, it is quite low, below 75 per cent, in Bihar, Rajasthan and Uttar Pradesh, and below the national average of 91.5 per cent in Andhra Pradesh, Haryana, Madhya Pradesh, Orissa and Punjab. At the upper primary level, gross enrolment ratios for girls range from a low of 20.7 in Bihar and 28.7 per cent in Rajasthan to 91.7 per cent in West

Bengal, 93.6 per cent in Tamil Nadu and 102.1 per cent in Kerala (table 19).

Enrolment at school does not necessarily signify access to learning opportunities, because of low attendance and heavy drop-out rates. Estimates based on the 1981 census data indicated that about one third of urban girls and two thirds of rural girls in the age group 6-13 years were then not attending school. Data from the Department of Education also show that the drop-out rates of girls at the primary as well as upper primary stage are higher than those for boys. Although the drop-out rates have been decreasing during the past three decades, provisional estimates for 1993/94 indicate that about 39 per cent of girls and 36 per cent of boys entering class I drop out before reaching class V, and that 57 per cent of girls and 50 per cent of boys drop out before reaching class VIII and thus fail to complete the elementary level of education (table 20). There is considerable inter-state variation in drop-out rates, these being higher in educationally backward states. Drop-out is usually preceded by absenteeism for short or long durations.

Table 19. Gross enrolment ratios at primary and upper primary stages for major states: 1994/95

(Percentage)

State[a/]	Primary stage (classes I-V)			Upper primary (classes VI-VIII)		
	Both sexes	Boys	Girls	Both sexes	Boys	Girls
Andhra Pradesh	92.7	98.0	87.1	48.8	57.1	40.1
Assam	129.3	134.0	124.4	79.7	92.4	66.4
Bihar	76.2	95.9	54.7	34.1	46.4	20.7
Gujarat	123.4	136.4	109.6	63.9	75.5	51.4
Haryana	87.1	89.8	84.0	64.9	73.1	55.6
Karnataka	122.9	126.1	119.4	71.7	77.1	66.0
Kerala	98.4	99.8	97.0	103.5	105.0	102.1
Madhya Pradesh	97.0	109.7	83.2	52.8	69.1	35.3
Maharashtra	121.7	125.0	110.2	83.7	91.9	74.9
Orissa	95.4	117.3	77.6	56.6	73.9	39.9
Punjab	90.2	92.7	87.6	55.0	79.3	28.7
Rajasthan	96.9	124.5	67.0	55.4	79.3	28.7
Tamil Nadu	148.4	155.0	141.4	103.4	112.6	93.6
Uttar Pradesh	89.8	105.1	72.7	55.4	73.1	35.3
West Bengal	121.9	124.0	119.8	96.2	100.6	91.7
All India	103.0	113.8	91.5	65.5	77.1	52.9

Source: Department of Education, cited in *Economic Survey, 1995/96.*

[a/] Major states include states with a population of 10 million and above as per the 1991 census.

Table 20. Drop-out rates at different stages of school education: 1960/61 to 1993/94

(Percentage)

Year	Primary (classes I-V)		Elementary (classes I-VIII)		Secondary (classes I-X)	
	Boys	Girls	Boys	Girls	Boys	Girls
1960/61	61.74	70.93	n.a.	n.a.	n.a.	n.a.
1965/66	63.17	70.49	n.a.	n.a.	n.a.	n.a.
1970/71	64.48	70.92	74.60	83.40	n.a.	n.a.
1975/76	60.21	66.18	74.30	82.80	n.a.	n.a.
1980/81	56.20	62.50	68.00	79.40	86.60	79.80
1981/82	51.10	57.30	68.50	77.70	86.81	79.44
1982/83	49.40	56.30	66.04	74.96	86.24	78.21
1985/86	45.84	50.27	60.70	70.04	73.97	83.16
1088/89	46.74	49.69	59.38	68.31	79.46	72.68
1989/90	46.50	50.35	61.00	68.75	77.72	70.99
1090/91	40.10	45.97	59.12	65.13	76.96	67.50
1991/92[a]	41.03	45.17	54.30	62.04	75.87	68.55
1992/93[a]	40.07	43.02	53.99	66.06	74.69	68.15
1993/94[a]	36.07	39.05	49.95	56.78	74.54	68.41

Source: Department of Education, Ministry of Human Resources Development.

[a] Provisional estimates.

n.a. = not available.

The relatively low enrolment rates and high drop-out rates among girls could be attributed to a combination of factors. The excessive involvement of young girls in domestic chores and sibling care prevents them from attending school regularly, leading to the ultimate withdrawal from school. Available data indicate that it is girls from poor households and lower occupational hierarchy as well as from scheduled castes and tribes who are more likely to be not enrolled or withdrawn from school. In general, the parents of these girls are illiterate or semi-literate and do not readily or easily appreciate the value of education for girls. Second, even though fees are not charged at the elementary level, most parents cannot afford the "other expenses" connected with the schooling of their children, such as uniforms, books and other learning materials, and transport costs. Various schemes to help children from poor families do not seem to reach the vast majority of the poor. Consequently, when the choice has to be made between educating sons or daughters, sons are inevitably preferred. Third, early marriage and cultural restrictions on the movement of post-pubertal girls act as obstacles to girls' education. The absence of separate schools for girls within walking distance is an important factor hindering female education, particularly in remote and rural areas.

(ii) Secondary education

During the past four decades, there has also been a rapid increase in school enrolment at secondary or high-school level, and this growth has been more marked in the case of girls compared with boys: while enrolments for boys increased more than fourteenfold from 1.058 million in 1950/51 to 15.011 million in 1992/93, the enrolment of girls at this level increased more than forty-sevenfold, from 0.162 million to 7.699 million, during the same 42-year period. Consequently, the proportionate share of girls in total enrolments at the high/higher secondary stage rose from 13.3 per cent in 1950/51 to 33.9 per cent in 1992/93, and the number of girls per 1,000 boys enrolled from 153 to 513 during the same period (table 21).

(iii) Higher education

There has also been a considerable increase in the enrolment of women students in institutions of higher learning. Available

Table 21. Growth in enrolments at secondary level by sex, percentage of female enrolment and number of females per 1,000 males enrolled: 1950/51 to 1992/93

(Thousands)

Year	Secondary level (classes IX-XII)			Percentage girls	Girls per 1,000 boys
	Both sexes	Male	Female		
1950/51	1 220	1 058	162	13.3	153
1960/61	2 887	2 340	547	18.9	234
1970/71	6 580	4 872	1 708	26.0	351
1980/81	10 794	7 593	3 201	29.7	422
1990/91	20 897	14 003	6 894	33.0	492
1992/93	22 710	15 011	7 699	33.9	513

Source: Department of Education, Ministry of Human Resources Development.

data indicate that female enrolment at this level was 16.64 lakhs at the beginning of 1993/94, and this figure represents an increase of more than four times the number of females enrolled at the time of the country's independence. It is clear from table 22 that the number of females per 1,000 males enrolled at various stages of higher education has shown a continuing rising trend for almost all stages and classes during the 10-year period 1981/82 to 1991/92. Females constitute a substantial proportion of total enrolments in the Bachelor of Arts courses and Bachelor of Education courses (where their share declined between 1981/82 and 1991/92), and in the Master of Arts and Master of Science courses. Although there has been an increase in the share of women enrolled in Master of Commerce courses, in 1991/92 they constituted less than a quarter of the total enrolments for the courses. Women are very much under-represented in engineering and architecture courses.

While females constitute a lesser proportion of total enrolments in all higher education classes, there appears to be a tendency for them to pursue disciplines or fields of study conforming more or less to defined female and male roles. Data from the Education Department clearly show that the number of females per 1,000 males enrolled is considerably higher in arts, medical and science courses, and much lower in commerce and engineering technology courses. This sex-typing appears to have persisted, although the number of females per 1,000 males enrolled has shown a steady in-

Table 22. Number of females per 1,000 males enrolled in higher education: 1981/82 to 1991/92

Stage/course	1981/82	1986/87	1991/92
B.A/B.A (Hons)	590	639	663
B.Sc/B.Sc (Hons)	374	448	452
B.Com/B.Com (Hons)	175	282	347
B.E/B.Sc (Eng)/B.Arch.	43	63[a]	95
B.Ed/B.T	880	769	829
M.A.	573	602	601
M.Sc	428	498	503
M.Com	89	172	239
M.B.B.S	350	474	533
Ph.D/D.Sc/D.Phil	380	497	495

Source: Department of Education, Ministry of Human Resources Development.

[a] Referring to 1985/86.

crease in respect of each of the disciplines during this period (table 23).

Although males outnumber females in regard to enrolments at various educational levels, available data indicate that a higher percentage among females compared with males are successful at various school examinations. For instance, the percentage of female students who had passed the examinations conducted by the Central Board of Secondary Education has consistently been higher for females than for males (annex table C.5). The significantly higher success rate among females clearly suggests that given the opportunity or access, females do as well, and frequently better, than males in education.

Table 23. Number of females per 1,000 males enrolled in major disciplines of university education:1950/51 to 1993/94

Year	Arts	Science	Commerce	Engineering technology	Medicine
1950/51	154	–	5	3	185
1955/56	195[a/]	–	7	2	189
1960/61	223[a/]	–	28	4	258
1965/66	369[b/]	–	49	22	294
1970/71	502	212	128	11	265
1975/76	558	273	168	18	229
1980/81	597	389	185	46	292
1985/86	667	479	281	81	416
1989/90	633	568	300	119[b/]	526[b/]
1090/91[c/]	655	583	316	122[b/]	521[b/]
1991/92[c/]	653	457	338	95[b/]	533[b/]
1992/93[c/]	647	480	359	119	524
1993/94[c/]	647	491	365	125	575

Source: Department of Education, Ministry of Human Resources Development.

[a/] Arts and science combined.
[b/] Only for degree-level courses; not postgraduate courses.
[c/] Provisional.

(c) Educational attainment

An important indicator of the educational attainment of a population is the literacy rate. In India, the censuses defined a literate person as one who can both read and write with under-standing in any one language.

The expansion in education that has taken place in the country over the years had re-sulted in an increase in the literacy levels or rates of the Indian people. Data from the cen-suses indicate that the literacy rate of all persons aged 5 years and over had almost doubled, from 18.3 per cent in 1951 to 34.4 per cent in 1971, and the rate for all persons aged 7 years and over was 43.6 per cent in 1981, increasing to 52.2 per cent in 1991 (table 24 and figure 6).

Despite the impressive increases experien-ced since 1951, overall literacy rates in India are still low compared with a large number of other developing countries in the region, and the pace of increase has also been much slower than in most other countries at compar-able levels of development. Further, the literacy rate for females has always lagged behind that

Table 24. Literacy rates by sex: censuses of 1951 to 1991

Census year	Literacy rate (percentage)			Male/female difference
	Both sexes	Male	Female	
1951[a/]	18.33	37.16	8.86	28.30
1961[a/]	28.31	40.40	15.34	25.06
1971[a/]	34.45	45.95	21.97	23.98
1981[b/]	43.56	56.37	29.75	26.62
1991[c/]	52.21	64.13	39.29	24.84

Source: Office of the Registrar General, India, *Census of India, 1991,* Paper No. 2 of 1992.

[a/] In respect of persons aged 5 years and over.
[b/] In respect of persons aged 7 years and over and excluding Assam.
[c/] In respect of persons aged 7 years and over and excluding Jammu and Kashmir.

Figure 6. Literacy rates by gender: 1901-1991

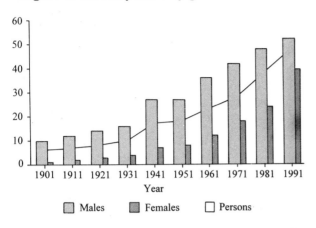

Source: UNICEF, *Children and Women in India: A Situation Analysis, 1990* (New Delhi, 1991).

for males, and by a big margin. There has also been no significant narrowing in the gender gap in literacy rates over the years; in 1991, the female literacy rate of 39.3 per cent was about 25 percentage points less than the male rate of 64.13 per cent. Roughly, the 1991 literacy rate for females is at the same level as that of males three decades earlier.

Moreover, the progress achieved in regard to the spread of literacy has also not been adequate in relation to the size and growth of the country's population. While literacy rates have slowly improved, the actual number of illiterates has been increasing owing to the growth of population and the backlog of adult illiteracy. The number of illiterates among persons aged 7 years and over was estimated at 320.4 million in 1991 compared with 302.1 million in 1981. Of the 320.4 million illiterates

in 1991, as many as 195.6 million, or about 61 per cent, were females, and of the 195.6 million illiterate females, 165.1 million, or 84.4 per cent, lived in rural areas. In other words, about 52 per cent of the total number of illiterates in 1991 were rural females (table 25).

There are also considerable inter-state variations in the literacy rates of the population aged 7 years and over. In 1991, Kerala State had the highest female literacy rate (86.2 per cent) followed by Maharashtra (52.3 per cent) and Tamil Nadu (51.3 per cent), as against 20.4 per cent in Rajasthan, 22.9 per cent in Bihar and 25.3 per cent in Uttar Pradesh. The 1991 female literacy rates were also below the national average of 39.3 per cent in Madhya Pradesh (28.9 per cent), Andhra Pradesh (32.7 per cent) and Orissa (34.7 per cent). The difference in female literacy rates between the lowest state (Rajasthan) and the highest state (Kerala) also increased, from 61.7 percentage points in 1981 to 69.4 percentage points in 1991 (table 26).

Literacy rates for both males and females are substantially higher in urban than in rural areas, despite the narrowing in these differences over the years. The urban-rural difference is also more pronounced in the case of females than males. According to the 1991 census, the literacy rate for rural females aged 7 years and over (30.4 per cent) was less than half the rate of 63.9 per cent for urban females. Further, the gap between male and female literacy rates is also considerably wider in rural compared with urban areas. It may also be

Table 25. Illiterate persons aged 7 years and over by sex and residence: censuses of 1981 and 1991

(Millions)

Residence	1981 census				1991 census			
	Both sexes	Male	Female	Percentage female	Both sexes	Male	Female	Percentage female
India	302.06	120.96	181.10	60.0	320.41	124.77	195.64	61.1
Urban	42.47	16.16	26.31	61.9	48.60	18.08	30.52	62.8
Rural	259.59	104.80	154.79	59.6	271.81	106.69	165.12	60.7

Source: Office of the Registrar General, India, *Census of India, 1991: Final Population Totals*, Paper No. 2 of 1992.

Table 26. Literacy rates of persons aged 7 years and over by major state and sex: censuses of 1981 and 1991

State[a/]	1981 census			1991 census		
	Both sexes	Male	Female	Both sexes	Male	Female
Andhra Pradesh	35.7	46.8	24.2	44.1	55.1	32.7
Assam	–	–	–	52.9	61.9	43.0
Bihar	32.0	46.6	16.5	38.4	52.4	22.9
Gujarat	52.2	65.1	38.5	61.3	73.1	48.6
Haryana	43.9	58.5	26.9	55.9	69.1	40.4
Karnataka	46.2	58.7	33.2	56.0	67.3	44.3
Kerala	81.5	87.7	75.7	89.8	93.6	86.2
Madhya Pradesh	34.2	48.4	19.0	44.2	58.4	28.9
Maharashtra	55.8	69.7	41.0	64.9	76.6	52.3
Orissa	41.0	56.5	25.1	49.1	63.1	34.7
Punjab	48.1	55.5	39.6	58.5	65.7	50.4
Rajasthan	30.1	44.8	14.0	38.6	55.0	20.4
Tamil Nadu	54.4	68.1	40.4	62.7	73.8	51.3
Uttar Pradesh	33.3	47.4	17.2	41.6	55.7	25.3
West Bengal	48.7	59.9	36.1	57.7	67.8	46.6
India	43.6	56.4	29.8	52.2	64.1	39.3

Source: Office of the Registrar General, India, *Census of India, 1991,* Paper No. 2 of 1992.

[a/] Major states are those that have a population of 15 million and above.

noted that while the gender difference in the literacy rate declined in the urban areas from 20.4 percentage points in 1981 to 17.2 percentage points in 1991, in the rural areas this differential remained almost unchanged during this period (table 27).

The gender differential as well as the residential differential in literacy rates also vary markedly across the states. In all 15 major states, male literacy rates are higher than female rates in both urban and rural areas,

but the gender differential is more pronounced in the rural areas. While the overall male-female differential for the country as a whole was 24.8 percentage points, it was lowest in Kerala (7.4 percentage points) and highest in Rajasthan (34.6 percentage points), and was more than the national average in seven major states. Similarly, the urban-rural differential in regard to the female literacy rate was 33.5 percentage points for the country as a whole, but this differential ranged from a low of 4.0 in Kerala State to a high of 37.9 in Bihar, 38.6

Table 27. Literacy rates of persons aged 7 years and over by sex and residence: censuses of 1981 and 1991

Residence	1981 census				1991 census			
	Both sexes	Male	Female	Male/ female difference	Both sexes	Male	Female	Male/ female difference
India	43.6	56.4	29.8	26.6	52.2	64.1	39.2	24.9
Urban	67.3	76.8	56.4	20.4	73.0	81.1	63.9	17.2
Rural	36.1	49.7	21.8	27.9	44.5	57.8	30.4	27.4
Urban/rural difference	31.2	27.1	34.6	–	28.5	23.3	33.5	–

Source: Office of the Registrar General, India, *Census of India, 1991: Final Population Totals,* Paper No. 2 of 1992, p. 51.

in Rajasthan and 39.2 in Madhya Pradesh. The urban-rural differential in the female literacy rate was also more than 29 percentage points in another nine major states. It is interesting to note that in most of the 15 states, the rural-urban differential in the female literacy rate was higher than the gender differential in literacy rates in both urban and rural areas.

A grouping of the 15 major states on the basis of their respective urban and rural female literacy rates is given in table 28. It is evident from this table and annex table C.6 that the urban as well as rural female literacy rates are low in the educationally backward states such as Rajasthan, Uttar Pradesh, Andhra Pradesh, Bihar, Madhya Pradesh, Haryana and Orissa. None of the 15 major states have an urban female literacy rate less than 45 per cent, and this rate is 65 per cent or more in eight of these states. On the other hand, the rural female literacy rate is less than 45 per cent in all states excepting Kerala, where both the urban and rural rates are over 85 per cent.

A classification of the various constituent districts in each of the 15 major states by level of rural female literacy rate is given in annex table C.7. It will be noted that of the combined total of 381 districts, the rural female literacy rate was less than 15 per cent in 73 districts (or 69.1 per cent), and was less than 25 per cent in 189 or about half of the total districts, and was less than 35 per cent in about two thirds of the districts. Data not included in annex table C.7 also reveal that the rural female literacy rate was lower than 10 per cent in 15 districts and lower than 5 per cent in two of these districts.

Age-specific female literacy rates from the 1991 census were not available at the time of preparing this profile, but data for earlier censuses from 1961 to 1981 indicate that literacy rates for both males and females are higher at the younger age groups and decrease with increasing age. For example, in 1981, the female literacy rates were 44.9 per cent for the 10-14 age group, 43.3 per cent at ages 15-19 and only 14.4 per cent for females aged 35 years and over. A similar pattern could be observed in 1961 and 1971, although at each age group the rates have been increasing over the years (table 29). These patterns and trends reflect the increasing availability of educational opportunities for the current population of

Table 28. Classification of 15 major states by level of female literacy rate in urban and rural areas: 1991

Urban female literacy rate (percentage)	Rural female literacy rate (percentage)				
	<15	15-24	25-34	35-44	85-94
45-54	Rajasthan	Uttar Pradesh			
55-64		Andhra Pradesh Bihar Madhya Pradesh	Haryana Orissa		
65-74			Karnataka	Assam Gujarat Maharashtra Punjab Tamil Nadu West Bengal	
85-94					Kerala

Source: Office of the Registrar General, India, *Census of India, 1991: Final Population Totals*, Paper No. 2 of 1992, pp. 210-214.

Note: Major states are those that have a population of 15 million or more.

34

Table 29. Literacy rates by age and sex: censuses of 1961, 1971 and 1981

(Percentage)

Age group	1961 census			1971 census			1981 census[a]		
	Both sexes	Male	Female	Both sexes	Male	Female	Both sexes	Male	Female
5-9	19.8	25.0	14.4	23.2	27.2	18.9	30.7	35.1	25.8
10-14	42.3	54.4	28.4	49.8	59.8	38.1	56.6	66.9	44.9
15-19	38.4	52.0	23.8	51.4	63.4	37.7	55.4	66.1	43.3
20-24	33.6	49.8	18.2	44.7	60.7	28.7	52.0	66.5	37.2
25-34	28.5	42.5	13.9	34.8	50.1	19.3	45.1	60.7	29.0
35 and over	22.2	35.3	7.7	25.2	38.0	10.7	30.2	44.6	14.4
5 and above	28.3	40.4	15.3	34.5	45.9	22.0	41.4	53.5	28.5
10 and above	30.1	43.6	15.5	36.8	49.9	22.6	43.5	57.0	29.0
15 and above	27.8	41.5	13.2	34.0	47.7	19.4	40.8	54.8	25.7

Source: Prabhash Prasad Singh, *Women in India, A Statistical Panorama,* Women in South Asia Series W 012 (New Delhi, Inter-India Publications, 1991).

[a] The figures are based on 5 per cent sample tabulation of the census data, and do not include Assam State, where the census was not held in 1981.

school-going age and the lack of such facilities for the older persons of today when they were of school-going age.

3. Health status

(a) Morbidity patterns

In India, a systematic analysis of the incidence of morbidity is rendered difficult by a lack of accurate and comprehensive data. While there is a large volume of data on the prevalence of particular diseases, it is not easy to arrive at an overall assessment of the disease burden of the country as a whole. Hospital statistics do not give a complete picture of the morbidity patterns as these data largely relate to serious cases and to those who have access to medical services and facilities. Health planners, however, reckon that at any given time 12-15 per cent of the Indian people are on the sick list.

Available studies and information also indicate that the health of Indian women is intricately related to the socio-economic status of their respective families as well as their age and kinship/marital status within the households. Given the predominantly patriarchal set-up, women and girls generally receive a lesser share in the intra-household distribution of health goods and services compared with

men and boys. Besides, owing to their involvement in arduous domestic chores and responsibility for cooking and feeding the family members, Indian women generally tend to neglect their health.

However, a study of levels and trends in the prevalence of ill health or sickness among Indian females is also handicapped by large-scale under-reporting of women's illnesses, particularly in the rural areas. Generally, females avail themselves of existing health facilities and services to a much less extent than males, and attendance records of hospitals and clinics invariably show a preponderance of males. It is well known that few women venture to visit a health centre, clinic or hospital if they can help it.

Area-specific studies also suggest that despite higher morbidity among women, more treatment is sought for males and a higher proportion of health services are provided for males. For instance, a study of primary health centres of Rajasthan State conducted by the Indian Institute of Management in 1982 reported a ratio of five men for every woman seeking treatment at these centres. Another study conducted in the same year in Uttar Pradesh State found that only a small proportion of females who were ill sought treatment from a public health facility, while the vast majority of them resorted to traditional remedies. According to a 1979 survey conducted in Madhya Pradesh State, over half of all current serious illnesses that were reported affected females, but treatment was sought in about half of these cases, and only 15 per cent of the patients went to a government health centre. Recent reports from various parts of the country, however, show a male/female ratio of hospital admissions varying between 2.1 to 1.0 and 1.3 to 1.0, the latter ratio being reported from the southern states. This gender disparity is even more pronounced in regard to in-patients compared with out-patients.

A combination of factors inhibit Indian females from using the available health services and facilities fully. Because of social barriers, women, especially from rural areas, do not usually go to males for treatment, and there are not enough women doctors in the rural areas. Besides, because of their household responsibilities, as well as out of ignorance, women tend to neglect their illnesses and do not seek treatment unless they are seriously ill. Further, clinics are often not open at hours convenient for women, and this difficulty is further complicated by the lack of suitable transport facilities in the rural areas and the socially required practice for young female patients to be chaperoned by elderly women when visiting a health facility.

Health is an obvious function of nutrition, and in India, gender is a significant determinant of nutritional status. According to studies carried out by the National Nutrition Monitoring Board and other interested institutions and agencies, the nutritional status of the generality of men, women and children appears to be low, but within this spectrum that of women seems to be poorer. Available data on dietary consumption among 1-18 year-olds show that girls consume much less than boys (table 12). A 1979 National Sample Survey also revealed that among women above 18 years of age, 60 per cent of those engaged in sedentary activity and about 70 per cent of those engaged in moderate activity had intakes below recommended levels. Various studies also show that the dietary intake of rural and urban women in

India ranges between 1,200 and 1,600 calories per day.

The food intake of women in low-income groups is substantially deficient in calories; dietary surveys show that the intake of these women is deficient by 500-600 calories and that this deficiency is more severe among certain occupational groups such as landless labourers, whose numbers are large and increasing. The shortfall in food intake in the poorer households is due to the seasonality of food availability. Food shortages become severe in the event of crop failure, drought, and fluctuations in food prices.

Although the relatively low nutritional status of women in India applies to all age groups, it is more acute among young girls, pregnant and elderly women. According to the 1979 National Sample Survey referred to earlier, over 75 per cent of pregnant and 80 per cent of lactating women in sedentary activity, and 100 per cent involved in moderate activity failed to consume recommended levels. By and large, women enter into marriage and motherhood from their pre-existing malnutrition and their health is further impaired by frequent pregnancies and childbearing. There is hardly any increase in intake during pregnancy over the pre-existing levels despite the fact that pregnant women in low-income families continue to remain active throughout their pregnancy. A study of poor women in India subsisting on a diet of less than 1,000 calories a day showed that nearly a third of the pregnancies were wasted in miscarriages and still births.

The poor intake of food and nutrients observed among Indian females is largely attributed to cultural traditions of intra-family sharing of food, which discriminates against females. This tradition, which is particularly rooted in the rural areas, compels females to eat last and often eat least, both in quantity and quality. Several area-specific studies show that chronic unemployment and underemployment, as well as recurring floods and droughts, aggravate this "entitlement failure", particularly among the poorer sections of society. A 1978 study conducted in flood-affected West Bengal, for example, showed that in times of economic crisis, girls suffer from malnutrition more than boys.

The most common manifestation of malnutrition is anaemia, which is estimated to affect more than 50 per cent of Indian women belonging to low-income families in the latter part of their pregnancies. The reported prevalence ranges from 40 to 50 per cent in urban areas, 50 to 70 per cent in rural areas, and nearly 90 per cent in those rural areas where hookworm infestation is endemic. A 1988 study conducted by the MS University, Baroda, in Gujarat and Mahavashtra States reported the following percentages of anaemic prevalence:

Pregnant women	Gujarat	Maharashtra
1st trimester	86	68
2nd trimester	92	83
3rd trimester	93	94

An evaluation by the Indian Council of Medical Research of the 10-year old national programme for the prevention of nutritional anaemia has shown that the prevalence of anaemia among pregnant women had not diminished and continues at a high level of about 87 per cent. Iron deficiency, the most important cause of anaemia in India, usually antedates pregnancy and is aggravated during pregnancy and labour. Repeated and rapid pregnancies and lactation perpetuate this conditions.

Nutritional deficiency is also reported to be widespread among infants and children; malnutrition, particularly of children, has been described as the disease of the poor. Data relating to the nutritional status of rural and urban populations collected periodically by the National Nutrition Monitoring Board in 10 states indicate that only 40 per cent of the children surveyed had diets which could be considered adequate. It is estimated that around 40 to 50 million children under 5 years of age subsist on a diet that is inadequate in terms of energy. The average deficit in the diet of a young child is reckoned at 350 calories per day below the estimated requirement of 1,250 calories for the normal growth and development of a 3-year-old child.

The four main nutritional problems concerning pre-school children have been identified as protein-calorie malnutrition, iron-deficiency anaemia, vitamin A deficiency and iodine deficiency. Studies of the nutritional status of pre-school children from socio-economically disadvantaged communities show that about one third of the children have a normal nutritional status and about one fourth to one fifth suffer from grade I malnutrition. Several micro studies have indicated a larger incidence of malnutrition among girls than boys and more attention by parents to the health of the sons compared with that of the daughters. Some studies, however, did not find any discrimination, either in the diet given to the girl child or in looking after her health.

According to the data collected for seven major states by the National Nutrition Monitoring Board, the proportion of children with severe malnutrition had declined from 18.0 per cent in 1975 to 9.3 per cent in 1989, while the proportion of children with normal weight status had increased from 2.9 to 4.9 per cent during the same period. The extent of severe malnutrition had also declined in all states, excepting Gujarat, where it increased substantially from 14.6 to 21.7 per cent, and in Orissa, where it increased slightly from 12.9 to 13.5 per cent. In 1988, the proportion of children with severe malnutrition was higher for girls than for both sexes combined in all states, excepting Kerala, Tamil Nadu and Andhra Pradesh (annex table C.8).

It is clear from the scenario described in the preceding paragraphs that the available data and information are too fragmented to give a complete and comprehensive picture of the incidence of morbidity in a country as large and varied as India. Nevertheless, the pattern of drug consumption as depicted by available data from hospitals and clinics, as well as common experience, suggests a heavy incidence of communicable diseases like malaria, tuberculosis, gastro-enteritis and thalamus, which together are estimated to account for more than two thirds of the illnesses in the country. Apart from these and the increasing load of degenerative diseases, there are a number of widespread deficiency diseases arising from the lack of nutrients such as iron, iodine and vitamin A. What is also known is that the prevalence of diseases varies with location, the seasons, literacy and income levels of the people, and other factors. Yet, certain illnesses like fevers, coughs, colds, headache, dysentery and diarrhoea seem to be prevalent in all areas.

A fairly accurate picture of the pattern of morbidity incidence in rural India could be obtained from the annual national sample survey of causes of death in rural areas conducted by the Office of the Registrar General, adopting the technique of lay diagnosis reporting by paramedical personnel of selected primary health centres. The data for 1981 and 1992 are presented in table 30; while male-female differences in general disease are not perceptible, female-specific diseases, particularly gynaecological morbidities, as well as those related to contraception use, sterilization, menstruation, menopause, and cancers of the breast and reproductive organs, add to the female sickness load. There is also a widespread tendency to treat many of women's illnesses as "normal" and attribute them to female biology. The concomitant secrecy associated with many women's illnesses conceals their actual incidence and also prevents effective prevention.

It will also be noted from table 30 that accidents and injuries, although not "diseases", appear to be increasing rapidly both among males and females and that in 1991, deaths due to accidents and injuries accounted for about 9 per cent of all deaths among males and about 8 per cent of all deaths among females in rural India. Available data (not shown in table 30) also show that accidents and injuries are the leading causes of death in the 15-24 and 25-34 year age groups.

Estimates by the Office of the Registrar General also indicate that the recorded data for all injury-related fatalities probably reflect only 20-30 per cent of the actual number of injury-related deaths in the country, except for road accidents and murder. A 1996 study also indicates that recorded deaths constitute about 23 per cent of estimated injury-related deaths in the country. This study also shows that in 1994 about two thirds of deaths due to injury among females occurred at ages below 29 years (table 31).

(b) Mortality levels

(i) Database

In India, a systematic study of levels and differentials in mortality is handicapped by a lack of complete, reliable and detailed time-series data. Although the country has had a

Table 30. Percentage of deaths by major cause and sex: rural areas, 1981 and 1991

Major causes	1981		1991	
	Male	Female	Male	Female
Accidents and injuries	5.9	4.1	9.2	7.7
Childbirth and pregnancy	–	2.2	–	2.5
Fevers	7.8	9.2	6.8	7.9
Digestive disorders	7.4	8.7	6.2	6.7
Coughs (disorders of the respiratory system)	22.8	18.2	20.9	16.3
Disorders of the central nervous system	3.7	3.2	4.4	4.4
Diseases of the circulatory system	9.8	7.7	12.0	9.8
Other clear symptoms	8.3	7.9	8.7	7.9
Causes peculiar to infancy	12.2	12.0	9.8	10.7
Senility	20.2	25.0	21.9	26.1

Source: Office of the Registrar General, India, *Survey of Causes of Death (Rural), 1981 and 1991.*

Table 31. Estimates of injury-related fatality: 1994

Age group	Percentage of deaths due to injury			Estimated injury-related deaths	Recorded injury-related deaths	Recorded deaths as a proportion of estimated deaths (percentage)
	Male	Female	Total			
0-18	27.3	33.0	30.2	243 025	29 914	12.3
19-29	25.5	30.3	28.0	225 321	66 984	29.7
30-49	29.7	21.8	25.8	207 618	63 865	30.8
50+	17.5	14.8	16.0	130 364	26 972	20.7
Totals				806 328	187 735	23.3

Source: D. Mohan and A. Deopura, *Accidental Deaths in India, A Statistical Survey* (New Delhi, Indian Institute of Technology Centre for Biomedical Engineering, March 1996).

civil registration system since 1876, the vital registration data were grossly deficient both quantitatively and qualitatively. Until about 1950, the area of registration in the sense of regular, albeit incomplete, returns covered only two thirds of the geographical area and three fifths of the census population. After independence, however, the area of registration was gradually extended to cover all the states and the statistical returns were becoming more representative of the total area and population. Nevertheless, even today the returns are far from being complete owing to substantial under-reporting of deaths as well as births. An important factor contributing to this deficiency is mass illiteracy and ignorance of the importance of reporting births and deaths. Besides, the scattered nature of the rural population and transport problems also discourage people from reporting the events.

Given the limitations of the vital registration data, attempts were made to collect the needed information through small-scale surveys. But these attempts were handicapped by the difficulty encountered by respondents in recalling all events during the reference period; and this recall lapse appeared to have been more serious in respect of deaths compared with births. In 1963/64, the Office of the Registrar General launched the Sample Registration System (SRS) designed to yield more or less reliable data for estimating vital rates. SRS, which was initially launched on a pilot basis, now covers the entire country, and provides for a continuous record of births and deaths from households in randomly selected villages and urban blocks.

SRS is a dual-record system, consisting of continuous enumeration of births and deaths by a part-time local resident enumerator, often a teacher, and an independent survey every six months by an investigator-supervisor. Discrepancies between the enumerator's record and the results of the survey are verified in the field, and the events reported by the two sources are pooled together for computation of birth and death rates. The base population required for computing these rates is also provided by the half-yearly checks. During the initial stages of implementation of SRS, the Office of the Registrar General noted that, "experience has shown that there is still some unavoidable under-count of events" and the resulting rates "suffer from under-enumeration".

Nevertheless, SRS is the best source of data on births and deaths in India, and estimates based on this source are used in this profile in addition to other sources, particularly national as well as area-based surveys and studies.

(ii) Crude death rates

Estimates based on the data collected through SRS show that the crude death rates for males as well as females declined from around 16 per thousand in 1970 to 10 per thousand in 1992 and that, since 1989, the female death rate was slightly lower than that for males (table 32).

The reported decline in the crude death rate during the past two decades could largely be attributed to a series of measures initiated and implemented by the government to improve the health status of the people, particularly women and children. For example, over the years the number of primary health centres and subcentres expanded considerably, thus providing increased access to health services and facilities in the rural and urban areas. The Integrated Child Development Services (ICDS) was launched in 1975/76, and since then the coverage under this scheme has been expanding rapidly. In 1992/93, the Child Survival and Safe Motherhood (CSSM) programme was launched as part of the overall strategy for improving the health status of women and children in India.

(iii) Age-specific death rates

The three-year moving average of age-specific death rates by sex for 1979-1991 and 1989-1991 based on the SRS data, and average for 1991-1992 based on the data from the

Table 32. Crude death rates by sex: 1970-1992

Year	Crude death rate (per thousand persons)		
	Both sexes	Male	Female
1970	15.7	15.8	15.6
1975	15.9	15.5	16.3
1980	12.4	12.4	12.4
1985	11.8	11.8	11.8
1986	11.1	11.0	11.2
1987	10.9	10.9	11.0
1988	11.0	11.0	11.0
1989	10.3	10.4	10.1
1990	9.7	9.7	9.6
1991	9.8	10.7	9.7
1992	10.0	10.0	10.0

Source: Office of the Registrar General, India, *Sample Registration System.*

1992/93 National Family Health Survey (NFHS) as well as from SRS, are given in table 33.

It is evident from table 33 that according to the three-year moving average age-specific death rates based on SRS data, there was a decline in the death rates for both males and

Table 33. Age-specific death rates: 1979-81, 1989-91 and 1991-92

Age group	Three-year moving average rates (SRS)				Two-year average rate (SRS and NFHS)			
	1979-81		1989-91		1991-92 (SRS)		1991-92 (NFHS)	
	Male	Female	Male	Female	Male	Female	Male	Female
0-4	41.0	44.8	26.3	28.9	25.3	27.9	23.0	23.6
5-9	3.4	4.2	2.4	3.0	2.5	3.1	2.1	2.5
10-14	1.7	1.7	1.4	1.5	1.4	1.6	1.6	1.7
15-19	1.9	2.8	1.7	2.5	1.9	2.6	2.0	2.9
20-24	2.4	3.7	2.4	3.2	2.4	3.2	2.5	2.7
25-29	2.4	3.9	2.7	3.0	2.7	3.2	2.4	2.9
30-34	3.6	3.8	3.2	2.8	3.3	3.1	2.6	3.2
35-39	4.8	4.5	4.0	3.4	4.1	3.6	4.0	3.0
40-44	6.8	5.5	5.5	4.1	5.4	4.2	5.1	3.4
45-49	9.4	7.4	9.0	5.9	9.2	5.7	7.5	4.7
50-54	14.9	10.8	13.3	9.0	13.3	9.4	10.6	9.4
55-59	23.2	17.2	20.7	14.0	20.7	14.6	14.7	9.9
60-64	35.5	28.4	31.6	23.2	32.7	24.3	26.2	19.1
65-69	52.3	41.2	47.1	37.6	46.7	39.0	33.2	28.0
70+	98.2	87.0	94.2	81.1	96.1	87.3	92.1	98.5
All ages	12.4	12.7	10.0	9.8	10.0	10.0	10.0	9.4

Sources: Office of the Registrar General, India, *Sample Registration System*; and International Institute for Population Sciences, *National Family Health Survey (MCH and Family Planning), India, 1992-93.*

females at all ages between 1979-1981 and 1989-1991, but this decline was somewhat more pronounced in the case of females than males. This declining trend has also been confirmed for most age groups by the average rates for 1991-1992 based on SRS as well as NFHS data. The SRS data also show that the death rates for females are higher than the corresponding male rates at all ages up to 29 years and lower than the male rates beyond 30 years. However, according to NFHS data, female rates are higher than the male rates up to age 34 and lower than male rates beyond 35 years. Data from SRS as well as NFHS also indicate that the gap between male and female death rates narrow up to ages 35-39 years and widen after 40 years of age.

(iv) Maternal mortality

In the absence of reliable data, past estimates of the maternal mortality rate for India had generally varied between 400 and 500 per 100,000 live births. According to the 1992/93 National Family Health Survey, the average maternal mortality rate for the country as a whole was 437 per 100,000 live births, the rate for rural areas (448) being 13 per cent higher than that for urban areas (397). The estimated maternal mortality rates for India are about 50 times higher than those obtaining in most developed countries of the world. But given the relatively higher fertility rates during the reproductive span, the actual risk of an Indian woman dying from a pregnancy-related cause is about 200 times greater than for a woman in a developed country. The rates for India also imply that more than 100,000 women die every year from causes related to pregnancy and childbirth in the country.

It has, however, to be emphasized that there is no figure of maternal mortality rate which can be considered reasonably conclusive for India because of the marked variations in this rate reported from different areas, regions and population groups. For instance, a 1984/85 study of data from 22 primary health centres in Anantapur district of Andhra Pradesh State revealed a maternal mortality rate per 100,000 live births of 545 for urban and 830 for rural areas. Several other small-scale studies have shown rates varying from 230 to over 1,200 per 100,000 live births.

In India, as in many developing countries, maternal mortality accounts for the largest proportion of deaths among women in their prime years. In 1987, deaths related to pregnancy and childbirth accounted for about 13 per cent of deaths among rural women aged 15-45 years, and 14 per cent of deaths for women in the 15-24 age group, that is, those women who are most at risk of maternal mortality. Recent estimates indicate that 15 per cent of deaths among women in the reproductive age group 15-45 years are maternal deaths. It is also estimated that for every maternal death, 13 to 100 women face severe life-threatening complications.

Studies conducted in various parts of the country indicate that maternal age and number of births have a strong effect on maternal mortality. By and large, women giving birth to children at ages 20-35 face much lower risk compared with women giving birth at ages below 20 or over 35 years. The extent of risk from this factor alone can be gauged from the fact that mothers aged below 19 years contribute about 8 per cent of an estimated 26-27 million births occurring every year in the country. It has also been observed that maternal illnesses and deaths increase significantly with the fourth pregnancy, reaching high levels after the fifth pregnancy. According to a 1984 survey, about 35 per cent of all live births in rural areas and 29 per cent in urban areas were of the fourth or higher order (table 34).

According to information on causes of maternal mortality as reported by paramedical personnel in rural areas for the period 1976-1992, the major causes are bleeding and anaemia, followed by sepsis, toxaemia and abortion (table 35). Severe anaemia, which, as noted earlier, is associated with malnutrition, is also one of the important reasons for abortion, premature births, and low birthweights. Despite the availability of broad-spectrum antibiotics, sepsis is still an important cause of maternal deaths in India. Toxaemia and sepsis reflect the inadequate health care actually available

**Table 34. Percentage distribution of live
births by order of birth: 1984**

Birth order	Percentage distribution of live births		
	India	Urban	Rural
1	26.91	29.40	26.23
2	22.05	23.99	21.52
3	17.74	17.95	17.69
4	12.63	11.43	12.95
5+	20.67	17.23	21.61
Total	100.00	100.00	100.00

Source: Office of the Registrar General, India, *Survey on Birth Order Differentials, 1984*, cited in UNICEF, *Children and Women in India: A Situation Analysis, 1990* (New Delhi, 1991).

to women in the antenatal, intranatal and post-natal periods. Even though abortion has been legalized in India as a health measure since 1972, mortality and morbidity due to "illegal" abortions remain a major problem owing to ignorance of the law as well as non-availability of professional services within easy reach of the rural women.

Most pregnancy complications and maternal deaths can be prevented if pregnant women have adequate access to good quality antenatal and post-natal care. The type of care received during pregnancy and childbirth is crucial for the health and survival of both mother and infant. According to the 1986/87 National Sample Survey, the percentage of mothers registered for prenatal care was 21 per cent in rural areas and 47 per cent in urban areas. The 1992/93 NFHS revealed that about 37 per cent of mothers did not receive any antenatal care either at home or elsewhere during the four years preceding the survey, and that such care was provided by qualified allopathic doctors for only 40 per cent of the pathic doctors for only 40 per cent of the births, and by other health professionals such as midwife/nurse, ayurvedic doctor or homeopathic doctor for another 9 per cent of the births (figure 7).

Figure 7. Source of antenatal care during pregnancy

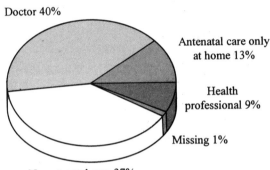

Doctor 40%

Antenatal care only at home 13%

Health professional 9%

Missing 1%

No antenatal care 37%

Source: International Institute for Population Sciences, *National Family Health Survey (MCH and Family Planning), India, 1992/93.*

Note: Based on births in the period 1-47 months preceding the survey.

**Table 35. Percentage distribution of deaths related to pregnancy and childbirth
by cause: 1976-1986**

Specific cause	1976	1980	1984	1986	1989	1992
Abortion	11.6	12.5	10.8	8.0	10.9	13.7
Toxaemia	10.4	12.4	10.8	11.9	7.9	12.6
Anaemia	22.1	15.8	23.3	17.0	20.3	19.6
Bleeding of pregnancy and puerperium	17.2	15.8	18.8	21.6	23.8	25.2
Malposition of child leading to death of mother	8.6	13.4	6.2	6.2	10.9	8.5
Puerperium sepsis	13.5	12.4	10.8	13.1	5.9	11.5
Not classifiable	16.6	17.7	19.3	22.2	20.3	8.9
Total	100.0	100.0	100.0	100.0	100.0	100.0

Sources: Office of the Registrar General, India, *Survey of Causes of Death (Rural)*, cited in UNICEF, *An Analysis of the Situation of Children in India* (1984); and *Children and Women in India: A Situation Analysis, 1990* (1991); and Department of Statistics, *Women and Men in India, 1995.*

The 1992/93 NFHS also showed that only 54 per cent of the mothers received two doses of tetanus toxoid vaccination, and 51 per cent received iron and folic acid tablets. According to that NFHS, about 59 per cent of mothers who received no antenatal care did not seek such services because they did not consider it necessary to go for antenatal check-up, and surprisingly this proportion was reported to be higher in urban (66.4 per cent) than in rural (57.6 per cent) areas. Lack of knowledge about antenatal services was the second most important reason stated by 13 per cent of the mothers who did not receive this care during their pregnancy.

Place of delivery and type of assistance available during delivery are also important factors contributing to levels of maternal mortality rates. Data from SRS indicate that, in 1991, about 54 per cent of all births in the country took place in the home, and were conducted by an untrained village *dai* or midwife or other untrained personnel. Only about 24 per cent of the deliveries took place in institutions such as hospitals, maternity/ nursing homes and health centres, and another 22 per cent in homes, conducted by doctors or trained paramedics (table 36).

The findings of the 1992/93 NFHS more or less confirm the information available from SRS. According to the NFHS, only one quarter of births during the four years preceding the survey occurred in medical institutions, and 74 per cent at home. The proportion of deliveries taking place in medical institutions was three and half times higher in urban areas (58 per cent) than in rural areas (16 per cent). The 1992/93 NFHS also reported that among deliveries taking place in the women's home, less than 3 per cent were attended by a doctor and 8 per cent by a trained nurse/ midwife (see also figure 8).

The indicators of maternal care discussed in the preceding paragraphs also differ markedly among the various states in the country. According to the 1992/93 NFHS, the percentage of births in respect of which mothers received antenatal care was almost universal in Kerala (97 per cent), Goa (95 per cent) and Tamil Nadu (94 per cent), but was as low as 31.2 per cent in Rajasthan and 36.8 per cent in Bihar. The percentage of mothers receiving two doses of anti-tetanus injections as well as iron and folic acid tablets was also higher in those states where the proportion of mothers receiving antenatal care was higher. The

Table 36. Percentage distribution of live births by type of medical attention received by mother at the time of delivery: 1980-1991

Type of assistance/facilities	Area	1980	1985	1988	1990	1991
1. Institutions such as hospitals,	India	17.4	19.9	21.5	22.9	24.3
maternity/nursing homes,	Urban	37.4	47.4	49.7	52.8	53.8
health centres etc.	Rural	11.0	13.3	14.9	16.2	17.6
2. Delivery conducted at home	India	16.7	18.7	19.7	21.3	21.9
by doctor, trained *dai*, trained	Urban	27.3	24.9	24.5	26.1	26.9
midwife, nurse etc.	Rural	13.2	17.2	18.6	20.2	20.8
3. Delivery conducted in the home	India	48.4	44.1	56.2	54.4	53.7
by untrained village *dai* or other	Urban	26.5	19.5	24.1	20.6	19.2
untrained professional functionary	Rural	55.4	50.0	63.6	62.0	61.5
4. Delivery conducted in the home	India	17.5	17.3	2.6	1.4	a/
by relation and others, excluding	Urban	8.5	8.2	1.7	0.6	a/
the above-stated category of persons	Rural	20.4	19.5	2.9	1.5	a/

Source: Office of the Registrar General, *Sample Registration System* (various years).

a/ Included in category 3.

Figure 8. Percentage distribution of live births by place of delivery and type of assistance during delivery: 1992/93 NFHS

Place of delivery

Assistance during delivery

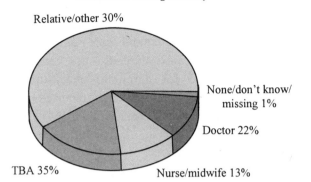

Source: International Institute for Population Sciences, *National Family Health Survey (MCH and Family Planning), India, 1992/93.*

Note: Based on births in the period 1-47 months preceding the 1992/93 NFH Survey.

TBA = traditional birth attendant.

proportion of institutional deliveries also varied, from a low of 11.6 per cent in Rajasthan to a high of 87-88 per cent in Kerala and Goa (annex table C.9).

(v) Infant mortality rate

According to the Survey on Infant and Child Mortality conducted by the Office of the Registrar General in 1979, the infant mortality rate for India averaged 219 per 1,000 live births during the period 1916-1920. Since then the rate had gradually declined to an average of 146 during the period 1951-1961. Data from SRS (table 37) indicate that there has been a further substantial decline in infant mortality rates during the two decades 1972-1992; during this period, the rate for males declined from 132 to 79, while that for females declined from 148 to 80. Consequently, the gap between male and female infant mortality rates deceased from 16 points in 1972 to one point in 1992. Despite these impressive declines, the current infant mortality rate remains at unacceptably high levels.

The national averages, however, mask the pronounced variations in infant mortality rates between urban and rural areas and between one state and another. In 1991, the rural infant mortality rate was higher than the urban rate by 34 points for males and 35 points for females. In many states, the female infant

Table 37. Infant mortality rates by sex: 1972-1992

Year	Infant mortality rate (per 1,000 live births)		
	Both sexes	Male	Female
1972	139	132	148
1976	129	124	134
1980	114	113	115
1984	104	104	104
1985	97	96	98
1986	96	96	97
1987	95	95	96
1988	94	95	93
1989	91	92	90
1990	80	78	81
1991	80	81	80
1992	79	79	80

Source: Office of the Registrar General, *Sample Registration System* (various years).

mortality in rural areas was about 50 per cent higher than the corresponding urban rates, thus bringing into sharp focus the rural-urban gap. The female infant mortality rate also ranged from a low of 16 per thousand live births in Kerala to a high of 123 in Orissa. The rural female infant mortality rate was 105 or more per 1,000 live births in Uttar Pradesh, Madhya Pradesh and Orissa. In urban as well as rural areas, infant mortality rates were higher for females than males in Bihar, Madhya Pradesh,

Rajasthan and Uttar Pradesh; in all other states the male rate was higher than the female rate (annex table C.10).

The hard crust of infant mortality rate in India may be seen in the three elements that make up this rate: perinatal mortality (0-7 days), neonatal mortality (0-29 days), and post-neonatal mortality (1-12 months). Information relating to these three dimensions as well as the still birth rate for selected years from 1970 to 1991 is presented in table 38. Unfortunately, these data disaggregated by gender are not available (see also figure 9).

It is evident from table 38 that most infant deaths occur in the first month of life (neonatal mortality), and the relative share of neonatal deaths in total infant deaths showed an almost continuous increase, from about 53 per cent in 1970 to about 66 per cent in 1990, but declined to about 64 per cent in 1991. In other words, today about two thirds of deaths among infants occur within one month of their birth. What is equally important to note that is that the fall in infant mortality that has occurred over the years has mainly been on account of improvements in post-neonatal mortality, the relative share of which declined from 47.1 per cent in 1970 to 36.4 per cent in 1991. In other words, there has been greater success in reducing post-neonatal mortality than neonatal mortality.

The perinatal mortality rate, which includes foetal deaths beyond 28 weeks of gesta-

Figure 9. Pattern of early deaths: 1976-1988

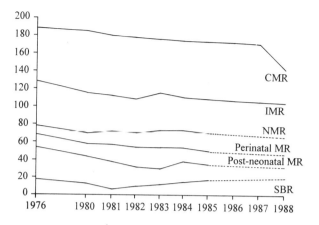

CMR   – **Deaths <5 years per 1,000 live births.**
IMR   – **Deaths <1 year per 1,000 live births.**
NMR   – **Deaths 0-28 days per 1,000 live births.**
Post NMR – **Deaths 28 days <1 year per 1,000 live births.**
SBR   – **Still births per 1,000 births.**
Perinatal MR – **SBR + Deaths 0-7 days per 1,000 live births.**

Source: UNICEF, *Children and Women in India: A Situation Analysis, 1990* (New Delhi, 1991).

tion, deaths of infants at birth and infant deaths within seven days of birth, is a sensitive index reflecting standards of health care prior to and during pregnancy and childbirth. It is evident from table 38 that the perinatal mortality rate has remained more or less constant, with slight variations from year to year. Although the still birth rate (included in the perinatal death rate) declined from 17.3 in 1970 to 10.7 in 1991, there appears to be a fairly high pregnancy wastage.

Several empirical studies have tried to identify the main causes of infant mortality.

Table 38. Mortality indicators for children aged up to one year: 1970-1991

Mortality indicator	1970	1975	1980	1985	1986	1988	1989	1990	1991
Infant mortality rate (IMR)	129.4	140.4	113.9	97.2	96.4	94.5	90.9	79.7	80.4
Neonatal mortality rate (NNMR)	68.5	78.3	69.3	60.1	59.8	56.8	56.4	52.5	51.1
Post-neonatal mortal rate (PNNMR)	60.9	62.1	44.6	37.1	36.6	37.7	34.5	27.2	29.3
Neonatal as percentage of IMR	52.9	55.8	60.8	61.8	62.0	60.1	62.0	65.9	63.6
Post-neonatal as percentage of IMR	47.1	44.2	39.2	38.2	38.0	39.9	38.0	34.1	36.4
Perinatal mortality rate	45.4	55.2	55.7	48.1	48.1	49.6	47.2	48.4	46.0
Still birth rate	17.3	17.6	11.3	10.4	10.2	13.5	12.7	11.8	10.7

Source: Office of the Registrar General, India, *Sample Registration System.*

Note: Infant mortality refers to deaths among infants under one year of age. Perinatal mortality includes foetal deaths beyond 28 weeks of gestation, deaths of infants at birth, and infant deaths within seven days of birth. Neonatal mortality refers to deaths occurring to infants up to 29 days after birth. Post-neonatal mortality refers to deaths occurring to infants 1-2 months old.

45

In the neonatal stage, prematurity, low birth-weight, delivery by untrained attendants, injuries at birth, tetanus, respiratory infections and diarrhoea account for most of the deaths. In the post-neonatal stage, deaths are often caused by tetanus, measles, diarrhoeal infection, diphtheria, pneumonia, bronchitis and other respiratory diseases.

Female literary has a positive effect on child survival. The relationship between the female infant mortality rate and the female literacy rate is brought out in annex table C.11. States with a higher female literacy rate have a lower infant mortality rate, the coefficient of correlation being – 0.758. The 1992/93 NFHS also revealed that infant mortality declined sharply with the increasing education of mothers, from a high of 101 per 1,000 live births for illiterate mothers to a low of 37 for mothers with at least a high-school education (see also figure 10).

The 1992/93 Survey also found that antenatal or delivery care by a trained health professional was associated with greatly reduced infant and child mortality risks. The survey data showed that the infant mortality rate ranged from a low of 44 per 1,000 for births with antenatal and delivery care to 64 per 1,000 for births with either type of care and to 97 per 1,000 for births with neither antenatal nor delivery care. The Survey also showed that infant mortality was highest among births delivered at home, followed by births delivered in public facilities; the lowest infant mortality rates were reported in respect of births delivered in private health facilities.

(c) Life expectancy

The female expectation of life at birth, estimated at 23.3 years at the beginning of this century, had risen to 58.1 years during the period 1986-1990. In other words, female life expectancy has more than doubled during a period of about 85 years. A similar trend has been recorded in regard to male life expectancy, which increased from 22.6 years in 1901-1911 to 57.7 years in 1986-1990. According to estimates prepared by the United Nations, life expectancy increased to 60.6 years for

Figure 10. Infant mortality rates by selected background characteristics

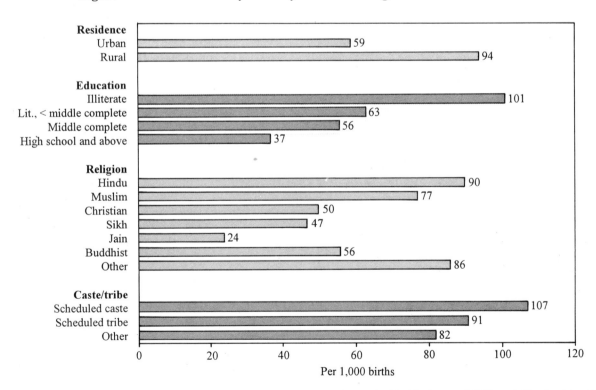

Per 1,000 births

Source: International Institute for Population Sciences, *National Family Health Survey (MCH and Family Planning), India, 1992/93.*

46

females and 60.3 years for males during the period 1990-1995 (table 39).

It is also clear from table 39 that life expectancy for females was slightly higher than that for males during the first two decades of this century, but lagged behind the male rate between 1921 and 1980. Since 1981, female life expectancy increased faster than male life expectancy and, during the period 1986-1990, the female life expectancy of 58.1 years was 0.4 years longer than the male expectancy of 57.7 years.

The expectation of life at birth by sex and rural and urban residence given in annex table C.12 shows that females have had a higher life expectancy at birth since 1970 in the urban areas, and from 1986 in the rural areas. It is also evident from this table that the rural-urban differential in life expectancy at birth has been gradually reduced, although this differential is higher in the case of females compared with males.

Table 39. Expectation of life at birth by sex: 1901-1911 to 1990-1995

Period	Life expectancy at birth (years)		
	Both sexes	Male	Female
1901-1911	22.9	22.6	23.3
1911-1921	20.1	19.4	20.6
1921-1931	26.8	26.9	26.6
1931-1941	31.8	32.1	31.4
1941-1951	32.1	32.4	31.7
1951-1961	41.3	41.9	40.6
1961-1971	45.6	46.4	44.7
1971-1975	49.7	50.5	49.0
1976-1980	52.3	52.5	52.1
1981-1985	55.4	55.4	55.7
1986-1990	57.7	57.7	58.1
1990-1995	60.5	60.3	60.6

Sources: Office of the Registrar General, India, *Census Actuarial Report and SRS-based Abridged Life Tables, 1986-1990*, Occasional Paper No. 1 of 1994; and United Nations, *World Population Prospects: The 1996 Revision.*

Note: Figures for the period 1901-1911 to 1961-1971 are based on census actuarial reports; figures for 1971-1975 to 1986-1990 are estimates based on data from the *Sample Registration System;* and figures for 1990-1995 are estimates prepared by the United Nations.

D. WOMEN IN FAMILY LIFE

1. The Indian family

In India, as in most countries the world over, the family is the basic social institution, although the structure or form of the family may vary from place to place or from one group of people to another. Traditionally, the extended family was the dominant family type in the country, and in its mature form, the extended household included the parents, unwed children, the married sons, their wives and offspring, and in some cases other miscellaneous relatives. All these persons lived in a single house, cooked at a single hearth, spent from a single purse and worshipped at a single altar. The extended family and its joint household performed important economic, religious and social functions, and was the focus of its members' most deepseated loyalty.

The head of the extended family was invariably the eldest male, who exercised full control over the family's resources and the management of the family affairs. All members of the family owed obedience to the family head and abided by his decisions. The interest of the family as a whole was deemed more important than those of any individual member, whose position and role within the family were defined by age, sex and relationship to others.

By and large, descent is traced through the male line, or patrilineally, but matrilineal descent traced through the female line is common in the north-eastern and south-western parts of the country. Under the patrilineal system, which emphasizes the continuity and solidarity of the male line, not only descent but also property and wealth pass in this line. From their birth, all males become co-owners of the assets of the lineage, each being entitled to an equal share irrespective of age or relation to the head of the lineage. Women share in the property only through receipt of a dowry at the time of their marriage. In terms of the matrilineal system, a man's legal heirs are the children of his sisters because descent is traced in the female line. However, in most areas, particularly Kerala, changes are occurring permitting a man's wife and his children to exercise a prior claim on his assets.

Economic resources mostly determine the extent to which families can approach the ideal of extended form. Generally, persons with substantial landholding and relatively large incomes from agriculture tend to live in extended households for a greater part of their lives. Among the wealthy, people generally live longer and extended families of good economic standing may include as many as four generations. Among the poor, as, for instance, landless labourers, only a very few families are of the joint or extended form. Strictly speaking, a small extended family no longer remains extended when the family head dies, since invariably the married sons set up their own household, which in course of time becomes a multigenerational household.

A major function of the family is to perpetuate itself through the production of sons; where sons are not born, it is customary in many areas to adopt boys from other families of the same caste or kinship group. Sons are considered important and desirable to continue the family lineage and name, to provide economic support to parents in their old age, and to perform the ritual of lighting the funeral pyres of their parents. Consequently, the birth of a baby girl is seldom a welcome event in the family; she is viewed more as a burden and a liability because investments in her bring no returns. On the other hand, the daughter has to be provided with an adequate dowry at the time of her marriage and this can be a heavy strain on the resources of most families. From the beginning, girls are taught to accept their lower status and the need for submission.

The strong preference for male children results in the girl child experiencing discrimination throughout her life, and existing sociocultural practices make it difficult for her to overcome the handicaps posed by her inferior status. Early in life, the personality and identity of the girl are stamped with emphasis on preordained feminine roles. Since she is a sojourner as a daughter, there is intense preparation in the socialization process for her to take on the roles of daughter-in-law, wife and mother. Particularly from the time she attains puberty, numerous restrictions are imposed on her as far as her movements and behaviour are concerned.

She is taught to observe restrained behaviour in speech, carriage, appearance, conduct, and interaction with males. Before marriage, she has to be well-trained in household duties and well versed in the behavioural pattern expected of a wife and daughter-in-law in the society.

Upon marriage, the young bride moves into her husband's household, almost as a complete stranger and into an environment where she is required to give obedience and respect to her husband and his family. She also comes under the watchful eye of her mother-in-law, who supervises not only her work but also her relation with the groom. The early years of marriage are generally the most stressful of a woman's life and this is particularly so if her husband works away from the village. Unmarried daughters living at home are treated much more leniently than the daughter-in-law. However, a woman begins to gain respect and status in her husband's home when she produces a child, especially a son.

The traditional family set-up and intra-family relationships are, however, undergoing gradual but significant changes on account of modernization, urbanization and migration. The movement of a substantial number of rural youth for employment in the cities or other areas is resulting in the break-up of the traditional extended or joint family system and an increase in nuclear families. Married sons are increasingly setting up their own households instead of living with their parents, and this has enabled young married women to be independent of the controls exercised by the mothers-in-law and other senior members of their husbands' household. In the cities where shortages of housing are severe, young working couples find it economical and convenient to stay with the parents. In such cases, greater autonomy is now exercised by the married couples. Several loci for decision-making exist in today's families, with the older family head functioning more through shared decision-making.

2. Household composition and size

The 1991 census data on household composition and size were not available at the time of preparing this profile. However, relevant data from the 1981 census presented in table 40 (and annex table D.1) show that the largest proportion of Indian households may be termed nuclear (categories 1, 2, 3 and 4) in both the rural and urban areas. For the country as a whole, about 54 per cent of the households were of the nuclear type in that they were single-member households, or households occupied by head and spouse only or head and/or spouse living with unmarried children. This proportion, however, was higher in the urban areas (58.9 per cent) compared with the rural areas (52.2 per cent). It is also evident from the table that the proportion of single-member households as well as households comprising only head and spouse is also slightly higher in urban than in rural areas.

The percentage distribution of households by size in rural and urban areas, as revealed by the data from the 1981 census and the 1992/93 Survey, is given in table 41.

It will be noted from table 41 that the proportionate share of households with 1-3 members had declined between 1981 and 1992/93 in both urban and rural areas and that such households constituted a higher proportion in urban areas (27.1 per cent in 1981 and 21.7 per cent in 1992/93) compared with rural areas (24.2 per cent in 1981 and 20.2 per cent in 1992/93). Consequently, there has been an increase in households with 4.5 and 6 or more members in all areas. In 1992/93, households with 6 or more members constituted nearly 4.7 per cent of all households in the

Table 40. Percentage distribution of households by type of household and area: census of 1981

Household type	India	Urban	Rural
1. Single member	5.80	7.91	5.15
2. Head and spouse only	3.98	5.28	4.91
3. Head and spouse with unmarried children	38.74	41.57	37.88
4. Head without spouse but with unmarried children	4.50	4.24	4.58
5. Head and/or spouse with/without unmarried children but with other relations	45.81	39.64	47.38
6. Other households not included above	0.17	0.36	0.11
7. All households	100.00	100.00	100.00

Source: Office of the Registrar General, India, *Census of India, 1981, Series I,* Part IV-AC.

Table 41. Percentage distribution of households by sex and area: census of 1981 and National Family Health Survey, 1992/93

Household size (number of persons)	1981 census			1992/93 NFHS		
	India	Urban	Rural	India	Urban	Rural
1	5.6	6.9	5.1	2.8	3.3	2.6
2	8.3	8.9	8.2	7.2	7.1	7.3
3	11.0	11.3	10.9	10.5	11.3	10.3
4	14.6	14.9	14.5	16.1	18.6	15.1
5	15.9	15.7	15.9	18.2	18.7	17.9
6+	44.6	42.3	45.3	45.2	41.0	46.8
Total	100.0	100.0	100.0	100.0	100.0	100.0

Sources: Office of the Registrar General, *Census of India, 1981;* and International Institute for Population Sciences, *National Family Health Survey (MCH and Family Planning), India, 1992/93.*

rural areas compared with 41 per cent in urban areas.

The average household size based on data from censuses and the 1992/93 Survey is shown in table 42. It will be noted that the average household size as reported by the 1951 census was smaller than that reported by subsequent censuses and the 1992/93 Survey in both urban and rural areas. The data from the Survey give a slightly higher mean household size in all areas.

Table 42. Average number of persons per household by urban and rural residence: censuses of 1951 to 1991 and National Family Health Survey, 1992/93

Year and source	India	Urban	Rural
1951 census	4.90	4.94	4.89
1961 census	5.16	4.97	5.20
1971 census	5.49	5.30	5.54
1981 census	5.55	5.45	5.59
1991 census	5.52	5.34	5.58
1992/93 NFHS	5.70	5.40	5.70

Sources: Office of the Registrar General, India, censuses of 1951 to 1991; and International Institute for Population Sciences, *National Family Health Survey (MCH and Family Planning), India,* 1992/93.

In India, males are conventionally reported as household heads because traditionally the father, and upon his death the eldest son, assumes the responsibility for management of the household affairs. However, some households report females as heads largely because of widowhood/divorce/separation/desertion or migration for long periods of the oldest male who would otherwise have been the head, or because of disability, illness etc. of the eldest male. Such households usually do not have sons old enough to assume the position of a household head. The censuses, however, report the de jure heads; the number of de facto female heads is possibly larger, especially where the women are the main providers.

The proportion of female-headed households as reported by censuses and sample surveys for the period 1961 to 1992/93 is shown in table 43. It is clear from this table that females constituted about 10·0 per cent, or less than 10.0 per cent, of household heads in the country, and that the proportion of female-headed households was slightly higher in rural than in urban areas according to all sources, except in 1992/93, when the urban percentage was reported to be higher than the rural one. It is also interesting to note that the proportion of female-headed households in both rural and urban areas had been declining between 1961 and 1992/93, except for the fluctuation in 1988.

There is considerable inter-state variation in the percentage of female-headed households. According to the 1981 census data presented in annex table D.2, the percentage of female-headed households was highest in the then union territory of Lakshadweep (34.36 per cent), followed by Goa, Daman and Din (23.25 per cent) and Meghalaya (22.23 per cent). Among the major states, Kerala had the largest percentage of female-headed households

Table 43. Percentage of households with female head: 1981-1992/93

Year	Data source	India	Urban	Rural
1961	Population Census	9.91	9.51	10.02
1971	Population Census	9.42	8.84	9.56
1981	Population Census	8.08	7.64	8.21
1984	National Sample Survey 39th round	9.40	8.68	9.64
1988	National Sample Survey 43rd round	10.24	9.92	10.35
1992/93	National Family Health Survey	9.20	9.60	9.10

Sources: Office of the Registrar General, India, population censuses of 1961, 1971 and 1981, National Sample Survey Organization, Report No. 351, 1989 and *Sarvekshana* Special Number, 1990; and International Institute for Population Sciences, *National Family Health Survey (MCH and Family Planning), India, 1992/93.*

(19.37 per cent), owing perhaps to socio-cultural factors and the substantially higher proportion of males who go out of the state for employment. The percentage of female-headed households was lower than the national average in several major states, such as Bihar (6.64 per cent), Gujarat (7.71 per cent), Haryana (6.32 per cent), Madhya Pradesh (6.46 per cent), Punjab (5.86 per cent), Rajasthan (5.27 per cent) and Uttar Pradesh (4.92 per cent). In general, the southern and north-eastern states had a larger percentage of female-headed households than the northern states.

3. Family formation

(a) Marriage customs and patterns

Traditionally, India had displayed a pattern of universal marriage among both women and men. Available data indicate that in the early 1900s, the prevalence was over 95 per cent and this high level had continued up to now; at the 1981 census, 97.7 per cent of males and 99.6 per cent of females were reported to be married by age 50. According to the Hindu philosophy, a male has to perform several sacred duties (Samskaras) in the course of his life, and marriage is regarded as the most important of all these duties.

The universality of marriage was achieved largely through early marriages, although the perception of right age at marriage had varied from time to time and from one place to another. Among the caste Hindus, for instance, pre-adolescent marriages were ideal for both sexes. Between 1860 and 1890, the "proper" age at marriage was deemed to be 8 for girls and 12 for boys; but the actual singulate mean age at first marriage reported in the 1891 census was 12.5 years for women and 19.6 years for men. By and large, the attainment of puberty has played an important role in determining the age at marriage for girls; Hindu society had strongly approved and favoured the marriage of girls before puberty or immediately after puberty. However, there were no definite social norms or taboos regarding the marriage age for males, but it was customary to have them married before they had attained adulthood.

The Hindu system and practices of marriage appear to have influenced strongly the marriage customs and values of other religious groups in the country, largely because a very substantial proportion of adherents of other religions in India were converts from Hinduism. For example, although marriage is considered a contract and the right to divorce is a significant aspect of marriage according to Islam, among Muslims in India, marriage has been practically stable. Pre-puberty and child marriages are also prevalent among the Indian Muslims.

In several areas of the country, an important aspect or manifestation of the early marriage pattern was the custom of child or pre-puberty marriages. Among Hindus, the motivation for child marriage was derived from the belief of divine sanctions against girls who do not marry before puberty, as well as against their families. Traditionally, virginity was highly respected and a qualification for a marriageable bride, and this is one of the reasons why even today parents are concerned and anxious once their daughters attain puberty. A further impetus to child marriage was given by attaching social prestige to such marriages; to have one's daughter betrothed before puberty was also considered a sign of one's affluence, influence or status.

As a rule, the procedure of child marriage was associated with a double marriage ceremony; an initial formal ceremony, which is more or less like a marriage contract, is followed some months or years later by a second ceremony at an auspicious time, after which consummation takes place. In such cases, there is a formal and effective marriage date, and age at first marriage pertains generally to the first ceremony, even though only the second leads to the formation of the family. Among some Indian social groups, betrothal has been taking place at birth and the marriage consummated soon after the girl attained puberty. Strong parental authority and family pressures were the explicit mechanisms for ensuring pre-adolescent and adolescent marriages of girls in traditional India.

Beginning from the early part of this century, there was social agitation against the practice of child marriage on two main grounds: the incalculable harm this practice causes to the girl child who was not yet physically mature for childbearing; and the very high incidence of child widows. These agitations resulted in the enactment in 1929 of the Child Marriage Restraint Act, commonly referred to as the Sarda Act. According to this Act, a child was a girl below 14 years of age and a boy below the age of 18 years. While the Act merely punished those responsible for bringing about child marriages, including even those who performed the marriage, it did not invalidate marriage below the prescribed age. Subsequent amendments have progressively raised the minimum age at marriage, which now stands at 18 years for girls and 21 years for boys.

The widespread practice of arranging marriages for sons and daughters is another important feature of the Indian marriage customs. Since marriage touches the reputation of the entire lineage and *fati*, it has traditionally been a matter in which the lineage elders and *fati* headmen have a considerable amount of input and say. Further, since marriages are contracted to preserve and improve the family's social status and its ritual purity, companionship and affection are of minor concern or relevance. The parents usually undertake the search for a suitable spouse for their daughter or son, preliminary inquiries and negotiations often being initiated at other marriage ceremonies. A careful, if tactful, mutual evaluation takes place, both families weighing their own relative merit against the standing of the family of the prospective spouse. More often than not, astrologers are consulted to determine the suitability of the match; go-betweens and marriage brokers have also been part of the marriage custom.

Until recently, two distinct systems of marriage were discernible in India: the north Indian system and the south Indian system. The rules of marriage according to the north Indian system were exogamous: spouses had to be unrelated in kinship reckoning and also very often by place of birth and/or residence. Since marriage was generally dominated by the search for inter-group alliances, women usually had no say and were more often than not married to persons whom they did not know. In the south Indian system, the rules of marriage were endogamous, with marriage among relatives, particularly between cross cousins, being the preferred form. Thus, females were more likely to be married to known persons in familiar households near to their natal home.

Another facet of marriage in India is the dowry; the custom of dowry in the form of presentation of gifts to the groom by the bride's parents or guardians has existed in India for ages. The dowry has normally been viewed as a way of compensating a daughter who is not given the right to parental property. The family considers it a duty to share gold and money and other utility items at the time of marriage of a daughter as a way to let her feel economically secure. The custom of giving dowry may also be rooted in the desire of parents to show affection for their daughters, who are married at a very early age. Whatever the reason behind this practice, it appears in many cases to have turned into a continuing cause for contention and harassment by the husband's family.

Over the years, however, there have been gradual but significant changes in the marriage customs, practices and patterns in the country. An increasing number of marriages are being contracted by the couples themselves with or without parental approval. Even where parents are largely involved in arranging marriages for their children, the changing nature of match-making to accommodate the preferences of the young are being considered more important than the actual survival of the custom.

Another important change that is taking place in nuptiality patterns in India, as in several other countries of the Asian and Pacific region, is the increasing tendency among women to refrain from early marriage but enter into marital union at a later stage. This tendency is evidenced by the rising proportion of never-married and the decreasing proportion of ever-married females at ages 10-29 years, as revealed by the data from the censuses and Sample Registration System for the period 1961-1991. This trend, which is noticeable in both urban and rural areas, is more marked in respect of the younger age groups than the older ones. The proportion of never-married decreases and that of ever-married increases with advancing age (table 44).

It will be noted from table 44 that the proportion of ever-married rural females aged 15-19 years decreased by more than half from 75 per cent in 1961 to about 36 per cent in 1991, but the decrease in the corresponding proportion in the urban areas was much greater, from about 52 per cent to about 16 per cent, or by more than two thirds, during the same 30-year period. There have also been significant declines in the proportion of ever-married females aged 20-24 years, from about 96 to 80 per cent in rural areas and from about 87 to 64 per cent in the urban areas. However, by ages 25-29, the vast majority of females have been married, although there was a slight decline in the proportion of ever-married females at these ages in both rural and urban areas between 1961 and 1991.

The tendency among the young to postpone marriage is also reflected in the increasing trend in the mean age at marriage. The singulate mean age at marriage for women, which remained at about 12 to 13 years until about 1931, has increased gradually, thereafter reaching 18.4 years in 1981, which is slightly more than the legally stipulated minimum age for the marriage of girls. Similarly, the mean age at marriage of males increased from 20.0 years in 1901 to 23.5 years in 1981, the legal minimum age being 21 years. According to the 1992/93 Survey, the singulate mean age at marriage was 25.0 years for males and 20.0 years for females (table 45).

Table 45. Singulate mean age at marriage by sex: 1901 to 1992/93

| Year | Singulate mean age at marriage (years) | | |
	Male	Female	Male/ female difference
1901	20.0	12.8	7.2
1911	20.4	12.1	8.3
1921	20.7	13.5	7.2
1931	18.4	12.5	5.9
1941	20.3	14.9	5.4
1951	19.9	15.4	4.5
1961	21.9	15.9	6.0
1971	22.6	17.2	5.4
1981	23.5	18.4	5.1
1992/93	25.0	20.0	5.0

Sources: 1901 to 1981: censuses of India; 1992/93: National Family Health Survey, 1992/93.

Table 44. Percentage distribution of never-married and ever-married women aged 10-29 years by residence: censuses of 1961 to 1981 and Sample Registration System, 1991

| Age group | Marital status | 1961 | | 1971 | | 1981 | | 1991 | |
		Urban	Rural	Urban	Rural	Urban	Rural	Urban	Rural
10-14	Never married	93.01	77.63	95.95	86.33	97.62	92.23	99.7	98.4
	Ever married	6.99	22.37	4.05	13.67	2.38	7.77	0.3	1.6
15-19	Never married	47.61	25.00	63.40	38.01	71.56	50.42	83.6	64.3
	Ever married	52.39	75.00	36.60	61.99	28.44	49.58	16.4	35.7
20-24	Never married	12.72	4.46	19.04	6.84	25.64	9.83	36.0	19.9
	Ever married	87.28	95.54	80.96	93.16	74.36	90.17	64.0	80.1
25-29	Never married	5.35	1.46	4.39	1.76	6.73	2.05	11.4	5.8
	Ever married	94.65	98.54	95.61	98.24	93.27	97.95	88.6	94.2

Sources: Office of the Registrar General, India, censuses of 1961, 1971 and 1981, and *Sample Registration System, 1991.*

It is also evident from table 45 that marriage ages have always been higher for males than for females, and that since 1961, the difference between the male and female mean age at marriage has been narrowing. However, even today females tend to marry men about five years older than themselves.

The national averages also conceal the variation in singulate mean age at marriage between the states and between rural and urban areas. According to the 1992/93 Survey, the female singulate mean age at marriage ranged from a low of 17.4 years in Madhya Pradesh to a high of 25.1 years in Goa. Among the states with a population of more than 5 million in 1991, the female mean age at marriage was reported to be higher than the national average of 20 years in Kerala (22.1 years), Assam (21.6 years), Punjab (21.1 years), Delhi (20.9 years), Orissa (20.7 years), Tamil Nadu (20.5 years), Himachal Pradesh (20.4 years) and Gujarat (20.2 years). This survey also reported a mean age at marriage for females of less than 19 years in Madhya Pradesh, Bihar, Andhra Pradesh, Rajasthan, Haryana and Uttar Pradesh. Similar interstate differences were also observed in respect of the mean age at marriage for males (annex table D.3).

Data from the 1992/93 Survey also indicate that overall both men and women marry at relatively younger ages in rural areas compared with urban areas, the urban/rural difference in average age at marriage being 1.9 years for males and 2.2 years for females. However, the average age at marriage varied from a low of 16.7 years in Madhya Pradesh to a high of 25.2 years in Goa for rural females and from 19.0 years in Nagaland to 25.0 years in Goa for urban females (annex table D.3).

The trend in rising age at marriage for females with especially large declines in marriage at very young ages is also clearly illustrated by the data from the 1992/93 Survey presented in annex table D.4. It is clear from this table that for the country as a whole the proportion marrying before age 13 declines

from 26.7 per cent in the 45-49 age cohort to 6.8 per cent in the 15-19 age cohort. While marriages before 15 years of age have declined considerably, marriages before the legal minimum age of 18 are still common. For instance, 54.2 per cent of women currently aged 20-24 years in the country married before age 18, this proportion being much higher in rural (62.8 per cent) than in urban (32.6 per cent) areas.

The median age at first marriage among women aged 20-49 years by selected characteristics estimated on the basis of the 1992/93 Survey is shown in table 46. It will be noted from this table that the median age at first marriage increases steadily from 15.5 years for women in the older age cohort 40-49 years to 17.4 years for those in the younger age cohort 20-24 years. At all current age groups the median age is higher in urban than in rural areas; it is higher among the more educated compared with the illiterates; and it is higher among Christians compared with Hindus and Muslims.

The changes in marriage patterns that have taken place in the country over the past few decades are due more to the changes that have occurred in the socio-economic status as well as in the cultural and behavioural attitudes of the people than to legislative efforts on the part of the government. The expanding opportunities for female education (and consequently the rising female literacy rates), and employment, urbanization and migration are also contributing to the changes in nuptiality patterns. As noted in table 46, age at marriage is higher among literate and urban females than among illiterate and rural women. States and regions that have higher literacy rates also have a higher mean age at marriage for women.

Despite the changes, early marriages and child marriages are still common in certain areas of the country. According to the 1981 census, about 8 per cent of children aged 10-14 years in the rural areas were reported to be ever-married. The 1992/93 Survey also reported that about 7 per cent of ever-married females aged 15-19 years at the time of the Survey had married before 13 years of age, this proportion being 8.6 per cent in the rural

Table 46. Median age at first marriage among women aged 20-49 years by current age and selected background characteristic: 1992/93

Background characteristic	Current age						
	20-24	25-29	30-34	35-39	40-49	20-49	25-49
Residence							
Urban	19.7	18.8	18.3	17.8	17.1	18.4	18.1
Rural	16.5	15.9	15.6	15.3	15.0	15.7	15.5
Education							
Illiterate	15.5	15.3	15.2	14.9	14.7	15.1	15.0
Lit., < middle complete	18.0	17.1	16.9	16.7	16.6	17.1	16.8
Middle school complete	19.1	18.7	18.3	18.4	18.1	18.6	18.4
High school and above	n.c.	21.7	21.4	21.0	20.8	n.c.	21.3
Religion							
Hindu	17.2	16.4	16.1	15.8	15.4	16.1	15.9
Muslim	17.2	16.4	16.0	15.8	15.5	16.2	15.9
Christian	n.c.	20.4	20.5	19.9	19.4	n.c.	20.0
Sikh	n.c.	20.4	19.6	18.9	18.8	n.c.	19.5
Other	18.8	17.7	18.1	16.7	16.1	17.7	17.1
Caste/tribe							
Scheduled caste	15.9	15.3	15.2	14.8	14.5	15.2	15.0
Scheduled tribe	16.4	16.1	15.8	15.6	15.6	15.9	15.8
Other	17.8	16.8	16.5	16.2	15.7	16.6	16.3
Total	17.4	16.6	16.3	15.9	15.5	16.4	16.1

Source: International Institute for Population Sciences, *National Family Health Survey (MCH and Family Planning), India, 1992/93.*

[a/] Median age at first marriage is not calculated for age cohorts in which fewer than 50 per cent of the women were married by the age that defines the lowest boundary of the age group.

n.c. = not calculated for reasons stated.

areas. Further, a 1984 study reported on the unlawful practice of early child marriage among low-caste communities in Uttar Pradesh State. However, the incidence of child marriage is reported to be diminishing, with parents and family members becoming increasingly apprehensive about their sons marrying girls who have not attained puberty or have attained it only recently, on the grounds that such girls are too immature to play the role of wife, mother and daughter-in-law.

It has also to be noted that, according to Indian marriage customs, the bride often returns to her parental home and does not begin cohabitation with her husband until after the *gauna* ceremony. This ritual usually takes place when the bride is considered to be mature enough to begin cohabiting with her husband. Hence, there is usually an interval or time lapse between the age at first marriage and age at first cohabitation and this interval is often long

for women who marry before menarche. According to the 1992/93 Survey, the median age at first cohabitation with the husband is about eight months later than the median age at first marriage. Since, as noted earlier, the median age at marriage has risen and early marriages have become less popular, the time between marriage and cohabitation has been reduced, and this difference is negligible in the urban areas.

(b)   Reproductive behaviour

In addition to changes in marriage patterns, there had also been significant changes in the reproductive behaviour of Indian women during the past four decades. In the early decades of this century, when mortality rates were high and the survival chances of children uncertain, women's fertility levels were high and they were exposed to the risks of repeated pregnancies. Age at marriage was then very low and childbearing and child-caring started from an early age of 15 years and continued all through the reproductive span up to age 45 or sometimes 49. Estimates indicate that an Indian woman then had, on an average, 6.7 pregnancies resulting in 5.6 live births, of which 4.5 survived. Thus, she had to spend a greater part of her reproductive years in pregnancy and lactation.

However, the situation in regard to women's reproductive burden appears to have been changing in recent decades, as evidenced by the reported decline in fertility rates. According to estimates based on SRS data, the crude birth rate, or number of births per 1,000 population, declined by about 20 per cent from 36.8 in 1970 to 29.5 in 1991, while the total fertility rate, or total number of children born to an average woman during her life time, declined by about 34 per cent during the same 21-year period. The decline in these fertility rates also occurred at about the same pace in both urban and rural areas, although the rates in rural areas have always been higher than in urban areas. The 1992/93 Survey revealed that during the three-year period 1990-1992, the crude birth rate averaged 28.7 per 1,000, while the total fertility rate averaged 3.4 children (table 47).

The decline in fertility that occurred in India during the past two decades is not as dramatic as that in several other countries of the region (e.g. China, Sri Lanka and Thailand)

during comparable time periods. Nevertheless, the recent fertility decline in India is quite significant in that an average Indian mother of today gives birth to about two children fewer than her counterpart two decades ago. The decline also implies that, given the necessary conditions, India could achieve a further substantial reduction in fertility within a reasonable period of time.

There are two important factors that have contributed to the recent fertility decline in India: increasing age at marriage; and decline in marital fertility or number of children born per married woman. Although analyses in respect of recent years are not available, a 1989 study (Retherford and Rele, 1989) pertaining to fertility decline between 1960-1964 and 1980-1984 reported that of the 1.06 point decline in total fertility rate (TFR) during this 20-year period, as much as 0.76 point, or about three fourths, were due to the decline in marital fertility, and only 0.30 points, or one fourth, were contributed by changes in female age at marriage.

Changes in marital fertility are largely associated with levels of contraceptive prevalence. In India, the contraceptive prevalence rate among couples in the reproductive ages is estimated to have more than doubled, from 10.4 per cent in 1970/71 to 22.8 per cent in 1980/81, thereafter rising to 43.3 per cent in 1989/90; provisional estimates indicate a rate

Table 47. Trends in fertility rates by residence: 1970 to 1990-1992

Year	Crude birth rate[a]			General fertility rate[b]			Total fertility rate[c]		
	India	Urban	Rural	India	Urban	Rural	India	Urban	Rural
1970	36.8	29.7	38.9	165.8	133.2	173.4	5.3	4.1	5.6
1975	35.2	28.5	36.7	150.4	118.6	158.6	4.9	3.7	5.2
1980	33.3	28.1	34.6	137.9	111.4	144.9	4.4	3.4	4.7
1985	32.9	28.1	34.3	138.7	112.9	146.9	4.3	3.3	4.6
1990	30.2	24.7	31.7	123.9	96.1	132.6	3.8	2.8	4.1
1991	29.5	24.3	30.9	119.2	93.3	127.2	3.6	2.7	3.9
1990-1992	28.7	24.1	30.4	123.0	98.0	133.0	3.4	2.7	3.7

Sources: 1970 to 1991: Office of the Registrar General, India, *Sample Registration System* (various years); 1990-1992: International Institute for Population Sciences, *National Family Health Survey (MCH and Family Planning), India, 1992/93.*

[a] Crude birth rate = number of births per 1,000 population.
[b] General fertility rate = total number of births per 1,000 women in reproductive ages.
[c] Total fertility rate = number of children per woman during her life time.

of 45.4 per cent in 1993/94 (table 48). According to the 1992/93 Survey, the contraceptive prevalence rate was 41 per cent among married women aged 13-49 years, and 40.3 per cent among those aged 15-44 years, which is lower than the corresponding estimates based on data from the Department of Family Welfare.

The contraceptive prevalence rate in India is relatively low compared with that obtaining in several other countries or areas of the region, such as China, Hong Kong, Islamic Republic of Iran, Republic of Korea, Singapore, Sri Lanka and Thailand, where the rate varies from over 60 to 85 per cent. Although the prevalence rate is modest, knowledge about contraception appears to be widespread in India. According to the 1992/93 Survey, about 96 per cent of ever-married as well as currently married women reported knowing at least one method of family planning, and 89 per cent of the women in these two marital status categories also reported knowing the source of (or where to obtain) at least one method of family planning. These percentages were also higher in urban than in rural areas (table 49).

Table 48. Percentage of couples effectively protected by various family planning methods

| Year | Percentage of couples protected by: | | | | |
	Sterilization	IUD	Oral pill	Conventional contraceptive	All methods
1970/71	8.0	1.4	–	1.0	10.4
1975/76	14.2	1.1	–	1.7	17.0
1980/81	20.1	1.0	0.1	1.6	22.8
1985/86	26.5	3.7	1.1	3.6	34.9
1986/87	27.9	4.5	1.4	3.7	37.5
1987/88	29.0	5.2	1.5	4.2	39.9
1988/89	29.8	5.9	1.7	4.5	41.9
1989/90	30.1	6.3	1.9	5.0	43.3
1990/91	30.3	6.7	2.1	5.1	44.1
1991/92	30.3	6.3	2.2	4.7	43.6
1992/93	30.3	6.3	2.0	4.9	43.5
1993/94[a]	30.3	6.8	2.7	5.6	45.4

Source: Department of Family Welfare, *Family Welfare Programme in India Year Book*, 1990-91, cited in Central Statistical Organization, *Women and Men in India, 1995* (New Delhi, Ministry of Planning, Government of India, 1995).

[a] Provisional.

Table 49. Percentage of ever-married and currently married women knowing any contraceptive method and knowing a source, by method and residence: 1992/93

| Marital status/ residence | Knowing method | | | Knowing source | |
	Any method	Any modern method	Any traditional method	Any method	Any modern method
Ever married					
India	95.5	95.3	38.8	89.0	88.6
Urban	98.5	98.2	48.0	95.4	95.2
Rural	94.5	94.2	35.5	86.7	86.2
Currently married					
India	95.8	95.5	39.3	89.2	88.8
Urban	98.7	98.6	48.8	95.6	95.5
Rural	94.7	94.5	36.0	87.0	86.5

Source: International Institute for Population Sciences, *National Family Health Survey (MCH and Family Planning), India, 1992/93*.

The age-specific fertility rates estimated on the basis of data from SRS and the 1992/93 Survey are shown in table 50. It will be noted that in 1970, fertility rose steeply from ages 15-19 to ages 20-24 to reach a peak at ages 25-29, and most of the fertility was concentrated at ages 20-34 years. But since 1980, fertility has been peaking at ages 20-24 and declining steadily after age 25, reaching very low levels for women in their 40s. Today, the Indian fertility scenario is characterized by a substantial amount of early childbearing, in that fertility is concentrated among women aged 15-29 years. According to the 1992/93 Survey, 80 per cent of urban fertility and 75 per cent of rural fertility are accounted for by women at ages 15-29 years (see also figure 11).

The fertility pattern discussed above is also confirmed by the age-specific marital fertility rates for urban and rural areas given in annex table D.5. The data do not show any significant declines at younger age groups 15-19 and 20-24, but there has been a marked decline in fertility in older age groups. It is thus evident that contraceptive practice is more prevalent among married women in the older age groups who have already had a number of children.

The percentage distribution of live births by order of birth and residence in 1991 based on data from SRS, and for 1990/92 based on data from the 1992/93 Survey, is shown in table 51.

It will be noted from table 51 that according to SRS data, nearly 57 per cent of all live

Figure 11. Age-specific fertility rates by residence: 1990-1992

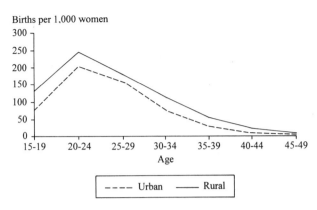

Source: International Institute for Population Sciences, *National Family Health Survey (MCH and Family Planning), India, 1992/93.*

births in the country in 1991 were of the first and second order, this proportion being significantly higher in urban areas (62.5 per cent) than in rural areas (56.0 per cent). Only about 11 per cent of births in urban areas and 13.6 per cent of births in rural areas were five or higher order births. However, according to data from the 1992/93 Survey, the proportion of first and second order births in total births amounted to 59 per cent in urban areas and 49 per cent in rural areas, and five or higher order births accounted for more than a fifth of all rural births and for 13 per cent of urban births during the three years 1990-1992. The 1992/93 Survey also revealed that lower order births were more common among younger women, while older women had more higher order births.

The percentage distribution of the 1991 current births, and of the second and higher

Table 50. Age-specific fertility rates: 1970-1992

| Age group | 1970 | 1980 | 1990 | 1992 | 1990-1992 | |
					SRS	NFHS
15-19	0.105	0.088	0.083	0.074	0.078	0.116
20-24	0.256	0.246	0.237	0.235	0.235	0.231
25-29	0.270	0.228	0.199	0.190	0.193	0.170
30-34	0.208	0.163	0.122	0.113	0.117	0.097
35-39	0.131	0.097	0.073	0.066	0.068	0.044
40-44	0.065	0.045	0.031	0.031	0.031	0.015
45-49	0.027	0.020	0.013	0.011	0.012	0.005

Sources: 1970-1992: *Sample Registration System;* 1990-1992: National Family Health Survey, 1992/93.

Table 51. Percentage distribution of live births by order of birth and residence: 1991 and 1990-1992

Birth order	1991			1990-1992		
	India	Urban	Rural	India	Urban	Rural
1	31.4	34.6	30.6	27.5	31.8	26.3
2	25.9	27.9	25.4	23.9	27.2	22.9
3	18.5	17.3	18.8	17.6	16.9	17.9
4	11.2	9.4	11.6	11.6	10.5	12.0
5	6.4	4.9	6.7	7.6	6.0	8.0
6+	6.6	5.9	6.9	11.7	7.6	12.9
Total	100.0	100.0	100.0	100.0	100.0	100.0

Sources: Office of the Registrar General, India, *Sample Registration System, 1991,* and International Institute for Population Sciences, *National Family Health Survey (MCH and Family Planning), India, 1992/93.*

order births occurring during the five years 1988-1992 by birth interval for urban and rural areas of India, is shown in table 52. According to the 1991 SRS data, the birth interval was less than 24 months for 38.5 per cent of all current births in the country, this proportion being slightly less in urban areas (37.3 per cent) than in rural areas (38.7 per cent). However, the 1992/93 Survey reported that only 26.9 per cent of all second and higher order births in the country during the five years preceding the Survey took place within less than 24 months since the previous birth, and that this proportion was higher in the urban (28.8 per cent) than in the rural (26.3 per cent) areas.

The 1992/93 Survey also reported that the median birth interval was 32 months, or about

2.6 years, and that birth intervals varied little by sex of prior birth, residence, education or caste/tribe. The median birth interval was relatively longer (35 months) among Jains and shortest (28.8 months) among Sikhs.

Although fertility had declined substantially in India since 1970, there are marked variations in fertility levels across the states and between urban and rural areas within each state. Data from the 1992/93 Survey show that fertility levels in 1990-1992 measured in terms of crude birth rate, total fertility, and children ever-born are below the respective national averages in all four states in south India and in all three states in west India; in two of these seven states (Goa and Kerala), the 1990/92 fertility was below replacement level in that TFR

Table 52. Percentage distribution of births in 1991, and second and higher order births in 1988-1992, by birth interval and urban/rural residence

Birth inferred (in months)	Current births in 1991[a]			Birth inferred (in months)	Births in the five years 1988-1992[b]		
	India	Urban	Rural		India	Urban	Rural
10-12	4.2	3.7	4.3	< 12	2.0	2.3	1.9
12-18	9.4	10.8	9.1	12-17	9.8	10.5	9.6
18-24	24.9	22.8	25.3	18-23	15.1	16.0	14.8
24-30	14.8	15.4	14.6	24-35	33.8	32.1	34.2
30-36	17.7	15.7	18.1	36-47	20.8	19.1	21.3
36+	29.0	31.6	28.6	48+	18.5	20.0	18.2
Total	100.0	100.0	100.0	Total	100.0	100.0	100.0

[a] Office of the Registrar General, India, *Sample Registration System, 1991.*
[b] International Institute for Population Sciences, *National Family Health Survey (MCH and Family Planning), India, 1992/93.*

was less than 2.1 children per woman. In all the other five states, TFR was less than three children per woman, and with a TFR of 2.48, Tamil Nadu was within striking distance of achieving replacement level fertility (annex table D.6).

At the other end of the spectrum, TFR was nearly four or more children per woman in Madhya Pradesh, Haryana, Bihar, Arunachal Pradesh and Uttar Pradesh. The 1990-1992 TFR of 4.82 children per woman in Madhya Pradesh was not only more than 40 per cent higher than the national average but also almost equivalent to the country's TFR of 4.9 in 1975. In all the other states not mentioned earlier, TFR varied from about 3 to 4 children per woman (see also figure 12).

It is also evident from annex table D.6 that fertility rates in rural areas are higher than in urban areas. While, for the country as a whole, the rural TFR of 3.67 children per

woman was about 36 per cent higher than the urban TFR of 2.70 children per woman, the extent of rural-urban difference varied across the states. Although in states with the lowest overall fertility, such as Goa, Kerala, Tamil Nadu and Andhra Pradesh, rural TFR was, on an average, only 12 per cent higher than the urban rate, in the remaining states the rate exceeded the urban rate by an average of 35 per cent, varying from 19 per cent in Orissa to 45 per cent in Uttar Pradesh and to 58 per cent in Jammu.

Apart from residence, the number of children born to a woman also varies in terms of other background characteristics, such as education, religion and caste/tribe. According to the 1992/93 Survey, TFR (current fertility), as well as mean number of children ever born to women aged 40-49 (cohort fertility), declines steadily with the increasing educational attainment of a woman. The Survey showed that TFR of an illiterate woman (4.03) was about

Figure 12. Total fertility rates by state: 1990-1992

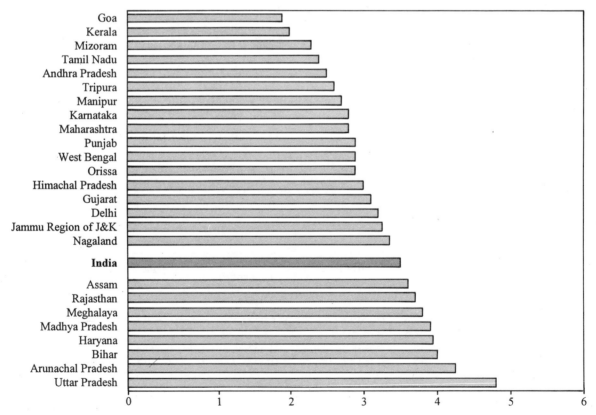

Source: International Institute for Population Sciences, *National Family Health Survey (MCH and Family Planning), India, 1992/93.*

J&K = Jammu and Kashmir.

1.9 children more than the rate of 2.15 for a woman with high school or higher qualifications. Fertility differentials by religion, though less pronounced, are still substantial, with the highest fertility being reported for Muslims and the lowest for Sikhs. The fertility of women from scheduled castes was higher than for women from other groups (figure 13).

4. Marital disruption

Persons who are widowed or separated/divorced are considered to be living in a state of marital disruption. Relevant data from the 1991 census were not available at the time of preparing this profile, but according to the 1981 census data, about 10 per cent of urban and 11 per cent of rural females aged 10 years and over were reported to be widowed, while another 0.4 per cent of urban and 0.6 per cent of rural women over 10 years were either divorced or separated (see table 16 above).

The very low proportions reported as divorced or separated may not be a true indication of the extent of breakdown of marriage

owing to under-reporting of these events. The incidence of dissolution of marriage through the formal legal system is rising in urban areas. Statistics on applications for divorce made in the courts and divorces granted are, however, not published. Data on the extent of desertion of wives by husbands are not available, though some studies have reported husbands having gone to other places for employment and not maintaining contact with their families. These factors have to be borne in mind in drawing conclusions from available data.

According to the 1992/93 Survey, about 3.1 per cent of all females aged 15.49 years in the country were widowed, while another 1.6 per cent were either divorced or separated. There were not very significant differences in those proportions between urban and rural areas. The Survey also showed that the proportion widowed increases with age from less than one per cent among women below 25 years of age to about 13 per cent among women aged 45-49 years (table 53). The very low proportions of widows at younger ages could be attributed partly to lower mortality

Figure 13. Total fertility rates and average number of children ever born, by backgound characteristic: 1990-1992

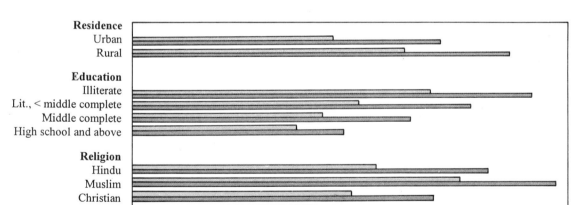

Source: International Institute for Population Sciences, *National Family Health Survey (MCH and Family Planning), India, 1992/93.*

**Table 53. Percentage of widowed, divorced and separated women aged 15-49 years,
by five-year age group and residence: 1992/93**

Age group	Widowed			Divorced			Separated		
	India	Urban	Rural	India	Urban	Rural	India	Urban	Rural
15-19	0.1	0.1	0.1	0.1	0.1	0.1	0.6	0.3	0.6
20-24	0.7	0.5	0.8	0.2	0.2	0.2	1.3	1.1	1.3
25-29	1.5	1.2	1.6	0.3	0.3	0.3	1.7	1.4	1.8
30-34	3.0	2.6	3.2	0.4	0.5	0.4	1.7	1.7	1.7
35-39	5.2	4.5	5.5	0.2	0.2	0.3	1.5	1.3	1.6
40-44	8.7	8.4	8.8	0.2	0.3	0.1	1.5	1.3	1.6
45-49	12.5	13.9	11.9	0.2	0.3	0.2	1.3	1.4	1.3
All ages	3.1	3.0	3.2	0.3	0.3	0.2	1.3	1.1	1.3

Source: International Institute for Population Science, *National Family health Survey (MCH and Family Planning), India, 1992/93.*

and partly to the greater likelihood of widows remarrying at younger age groups. The proportion reported as separated was about four times that reported as divorced in both urban and rural areas.

E. WOMEN IN ECONOMIC LIFE

1. Background

Indian women have generally engaged in economic activity, thereby contributing significantly to household income as well as to the national economy. However, the pattern of women's participation in economic activities outside the home is a complex one and varies according to geographic region, caste and social class.

The non-participation of women in the labour force has traditionally been regarded as one of the most important symbols of high economic and social status throughout Indian society. Socio-cultural norms had by and large restricted the role of women to the bearing and rearing of children and attending to household chores; they were not expected to involve themselves in work outside the home. The highest prestige was assigned to conventional domestic work for the family inside the home, while the collection of fuel and fodder carried a somewhat lower prestige. A woman working as an unpaid family labourer in her family's farm was more socially acceptable than a

woman working in the same field as a paid or waged labourer. The lowest value was attached to manual work for others as it necessitated not only a woman's physical presence in the public sphere but also her involvement in market transactions (Bennett, 1992).

A 1975 study noted a definite trend towards increasing female participation in work outside the home as one moved from north to south and from east to west on the Indian subcontinent (Gulati, 1975). This finding was also confirmed by another study undertaken in 1983 (Dyson and Moore). It has also been reported that this variation is not influenced by the geographic specificity of growing any cereals or rice. To a large extent, it appears to be related to the practice of purdah; restrictions on female personal movements and contacts with strangers are more strictly observed in the north than in the south (figure 14). Female literacy rates are also comparatively lower in north than in south India.

Several studies have also reported a strong correlation between caste membership and the activity of women outside the home. In general, lower caste women are engaged more in work outside the home than are women belonging to higher castes. It has been observed that, among lower castes, women are "partners of their husbands in the whole daily struggle for living" (Bhatty, 1975). A 1977 comparative study of women's work participation among three different castes in Rajasthan showed

Figure 14. Observance of purdah in the family by region and state

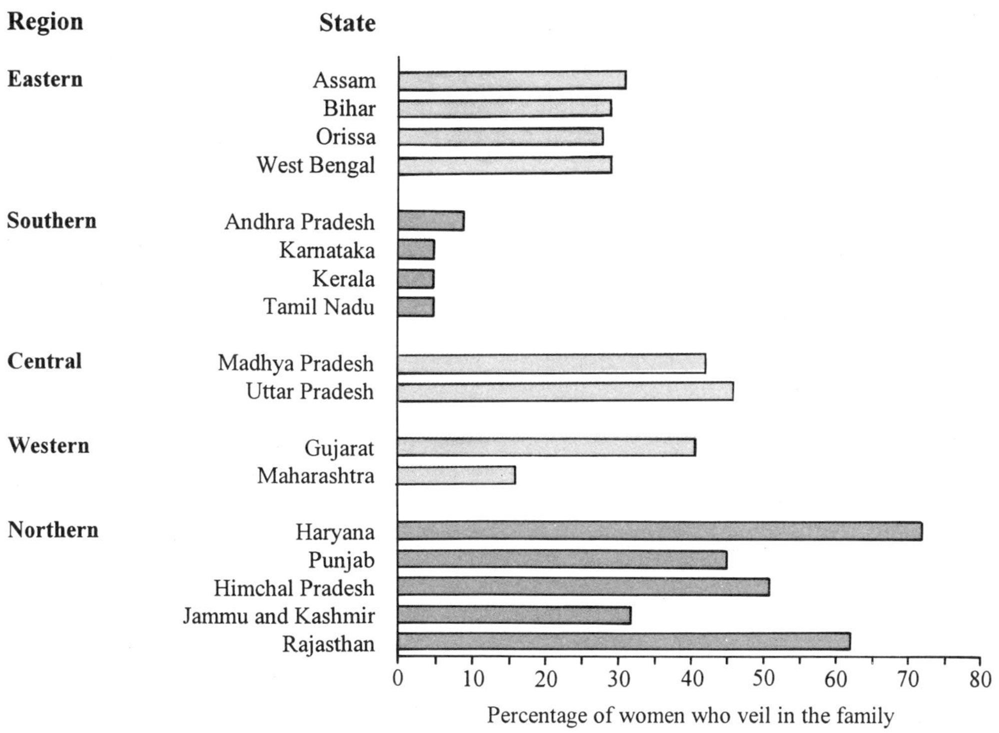

Region	State
Eastern	Assam, Bihar, Orissa, West Bengal
Southern	Andhra Pradesh, Karnataka, Kerala, Tamil Nadu
Central	Madhya Pradesh, Uttar Pradesh
Western	Gujarat, Maharashtra
Northern	Haryana, Punjab, Himchal Pradesh, Jammu and Kashmir, Rajasthan

Percentage of women who veil in the family

Source: Lynn Bennett, *Women, Poverty and Productivity in India,* EDI Seminar Paper No. 43 (World Bank, Washington D.C., 1992).

that while women from farmer/cultivator and untouchable families worked in the fields and in paid employment in factories, Brahmin women "did little more than cook elaborate dishes for their husbands" (Nath, 1977).

Available data and information also clearly indicate that the poorer the family, the greater its dependence on the economic productivity of women. Several studies have shown conclusively that the earnings of women account for a substantial proportion of aggregate incomes of poor households. These studies have also shown that the labour-force participation of women and their proportional contribution to total family income are the highest in households with the lowest economic status. The actual practice of purdah or female seclusion is rigidly observed only by the relatively wealthy families; among the poor, women have always entered the labour force whenever employment opportunities were available. Empirical studies also indicate that the poorer the household, the greater the probability of its women working as wage labourers rather than as somewhat more prestigious unpaid family workers.

2. Data limitations

Although women workers constitute a vital and productive sector of the Indian economy, and the majority of them work for long hours at home and outside the home, their contribution to production and growth has not been adequately accounted for in labour statistics. For example, the 1981 census reported that only 16 per cent of rural women in working ages were economically active, the corresponding proportion for men being 53 per cent. According to the 1983 National Sample Survey, 29 per cent of females as against 61 per cent of males in working ages were engaged in work defined as economically productive in the rural areas. In other words, according to data from censuses and sample surveys, women constitute only about a third of the national labour force.

The considerable under-reporting of women's participation in economic activities is largely attributed to the "statistical purdah" imposed by existing methods of measurement, which renders invisible much of the work performed by women. The issue of reporting women as workers devolves on the definition of what constitutes work or economic activity. Time allocation studies show that women are busy for longer hours than men and spend a considerable proportion of their time and effort in the collection of fuel, fodder and vegetables, which are either for direct consumption by the family or are sold to meet the family's other needs. Studies also show that women help in family occupations like dairying, poultry-rearing, raising and maintenance of kitchen gardens, sewing, weaving and similar subsistence-level occupations, and spend considerable time on the family farm and in taking care of the cattle at home. Nevertheless, such activities are often not reckoned as work because they are not marketable in an agro-economic system, although they would fetch a price in an urban industrial system. Besides, women's work is usually "invisible" because it is located in the domestic sphere, and as a rule, household tasks defy quantification and monetary valuation.

There is also a tendency among census enumerators and survey investigators to consider or treat as not economically active certain categories of workers such as unpaid family helpers, persons who work intermittently, seasonally, part-time or in subsistence-type activities outside the market sector; and most persons belonging to these work categories are women. Further, female participation rates tend to be understated because female respondents themselves do not very often consider household work as productive work. Thus, misconceptions and prejudices about women's input into economic production have been frequent and consequently much of their contribution had gone unnoticed by planners and policy makers.

In order to rectify the anomalies and omissions, the 1991 census altered the key question "did you work any time at all last year" to include the clause "including unpaid work on farm or family enterprise", and the census enumerators were instructed to classify seasonal, part-time and unpaid labour under the economically active category so that their contributions become visible in the labour-force data. Consequently, as will be noted later, the data from the 1991 census gave a better reflection of the work participation rates of women in the country.

3. Work participation rates

The trend in the work participation rate (or proportion of total workers to population) as revealed by the data of the 1971, 1981 and 1991 censuses is shown in table 54.

It will be noted from table 54 that, while for the country as a whole the overall work participation rate had risen from 34.2 per cent in 1971 to 37.7 per cent in 1991, the increase has been more pronounced for females than

Table 54. Work participation rates by residence and sex: censuses of 1971, 1981 and 1991

Residence	Census year	Both sexes	Male	Female
India	1971	34.17	52.75	14.22
	1981	36.70	52.62	19.67
	1991	37.68	51.56	22.73
Urban	1971	29.61	48.88	7.18
	1981	29.99	49.06	8.31
	1991	30.44	48.95	9.74
Rural	1971	35.55	53.78	15.92
	1981	38.79	53.77	23.06
	1991	40.24	52.50	27.20

Source: Office of the Registrar General, India, *Census of India, 1991, Series I, India,* Paper No. 3 of 1991.

Notes: Excluding Assam, where the 1981 census could not be held, and Jammu and Kashmir, where the 1991 census was not held.

The 1971 census figures include workers and non-workers with secondary work.

The 1981 and 1991 census figures include main workers and marginal workers.

for males, and in rural areas more than in urban areas. During the 20-year period 1971-1991, while the female work participation rate had increased by 8.5 percentage points, there was a slight decline in the rate for males. Further, the participation rate for rural females had increased by about 11 percentage points, but by only 2.6 percentage points for urban females. Despite these significant changes, the 1991 female work participation rates were considerably lower than the male rates in both the urban and rural areas.

The overall work participation rates given in table 54 are aggregate measures in that they give the level of participation of the total population irrespective of age. A clearer picture of the pattern of work participation is obtained by examining the age-specific participation rates. Unfortunately, these rates, based on the data from the latest census held in 1991, were not available at the time of preparing this profile. However, the relevant data obtained from the 1987/88 round of the National Sample Survey are given in table 55.

It is evident from table 55 that the female work participation rates are considerably lower than the corresponding rates for males at all age groups in both the urban and rural areas. The rates for both males and females rise steeply from a low at ages 5-14 reaching a peak at ages 30-44 years. Thereafter, the rates decline, but at a faster rate for females than for males, indicating that females more than males tend to withdraw from the labour force after age 50. The gender gap in work participation is more marked at ages 60 and above, the male rate being about five times the female rate in urban areas and four times the female rate in rural areas. It is also evident from table 55 that the participation rates for rural females are, by and large, twice the corresponding rates for urban females at all ages, reflecting the greater chances for female employment in rural than in urban areas.

4. Work categories

The Indian censuses make a distinction between main workers and marginal workers. Main workers are defined as those who have worked for a major part of the year, while marginal workers are those who have worked for less than six months during the year. The percentage distribution of all workers by these two work categories and by sex in rural as well as urban areas is shown in table 56.

It will be noted from this table that between 1981 and 1991 the proportionate share of main workers among females increased from 87.5 to 88.6 per cent in urban areas, and from 69.0 to 70.5 per cent in rural areas. Yet in 1991, about 28 per cent of all female workers in the country were categorized as marginal workers, the corresponding proportion among male workers being only about 2 per cent. The proportion of marginal workers among females in rural areas (29.5 per cent) was more than twice the proportion in urban areas. Thus, in India, not only is the women's workforce participation rate considerably lower than that for men, but a very significant proportion

Table 55. Work participation rates by age, sex and residence: 1987-1988

Age group	Urban areas		Rural areas	
	Male	Female	Male	Female
5-14	4.2	2.4	7.4	6.3
15-29	69.7	17.2	79.7	36.9
30-44	98.7	23.9	98.7	47.6
45-59	93.1	22.4	95.7	42.2
60+	46.6	9.3	64.9	16.3
All ages	59.6	14.6	61.4	29.2

Source: National Sample Survey Organization, New Delhi.

65

Table 56. Percentage distribution of workers by work category, sex and residence:
censuses of 1981 and 1991

Census year	Work category	India			Urban areas			Rural areas		
		Both sexes	Male	Female	Both sexes	Male	Female	Both sexes	Male	Female
1981	Main workers	91.0	98.0	70.8	97.4	98.9	87.5	89.4	97.8	69.0
	Marginal workers	9.0	2.0	29.2	2.6	1.1	12.5	10.6	2.2	31.0
	All workers	100.0	100.0	100.0	100.0	100.0	100.0	100.0	100.0	100.0
1991	Main workers	90.6	98.1	72.4	97.3	98.9	88.6	88.9	97.8	70.5
	Marginal workers	9.4	1.9	27.6	2.7	1.1	11.4	11.1	2.2	29.5
	All workers	100.0	100.0	100.0	100.0	100.0	100.0	100.0	100.0	100.0

Source: Office of the Registrar General, India, *Census of India, 1991, Series I, India,* Paper No. 3 of 1991.

Note: The figures for 1981 exclude Assam and those for 1991 exclude Jammu and Kashmir.

of women workers also belong to the category of marginal workers. Available data also indicate that in 1991, women accounted for 90 per cent of all marginal workers in the country.

The percentage distribution of main workers by major industrial sector and by sex and residence for census years 1981 and 1991 is shown in annex table E.1. It will be noted that in India most workers, both among males and females, are employed in the agricultural and allied industrial sectors, but that this proportion is significantly higher among females than males in rural as well as urban areas. For instance, in 1991, the proportion of all female main workers engaged in the agricul-

tural sector (including livestock, forestry, fishing and hunting) was 80.7 per cent, or 20 percentage points higher than the corresponding proportion for males. In the rural areas, nearly 90 per cent of female workers were employed in agriculture and allied activities, compared with about 80 per cent among males.

The percentage distribution of main workers by four broad industrial activities in 1981 and 1991 is given in table 57.

It is clear from table 57 that there was a change in the pattern of activity of females between 1981 and 1991. During this intercensal period, while the proportion of women

Table 57. Percentage distribution of main workers by broad industrial category,
sex and residence: censuses of 1981 and 1991

Residence	Sex	Cultivators		Agricultural labourers		Household industry		Other	
		1981	1991	1981	1991	1981	1991	1981	1991
India	Both sexes	41.45	38.43	25.12	26.49	3.45	3.66	29.98	31.42
	Male	43.58	39.72	19.71	21.11	3.17	3.37	33.54	35.80
	Female	33.09	34.15	46.34	44.29	4.57	4.62	16.00	16.94
Urban	Both sexes	5.11	5.00	6.08	6.71	4.91	5.59	89.30	82.70
	Male	5.17	4.92	4.68	5.40	4.18	4.83	85.97	84.85
	Female	4.63	5.54	16.65	15.00	10.44	10.30	68.28	69.16
Rural	Both sexes	50.95	48.22	30.09	32.29	3.07	3.10	15.89	16.39
	Male	55.03	51.61	24.19	26.49	2.86	2.87	17.92	19.04
	Female	36.94	38.58	50.36	48.30	3.77	3.75	8.93	8.84

Source: Census of India, 1991, cited in Devendra B. Gupta and others, *Population Change, Development and Women's Role and Status in India* (Asian Population Studies Series No. 132, 1995).

employed as agricultural labourers declined by two percentage points from 46.3 to 44.3 per cent, that of women engaged as cultivators increased significantly from 33.1 to 34.2 per cent. These shifts had occurred in rural as well as in urban areas. The proportion of females working in household-based industries, however, remained almost unchanged at about 4.6 per cent in both census years; this proportion in urban areas (over 10 per cent) was more than twice that in rural areas (about 4 per cent). The proportion of persons in the category of "other" workers increased by less than one percentage point for females compared with 2.26 percentage points for males.

It is also interesting to note that the percentage increase in main workers during the decade 1981-1991 was significantly higher for females than for males in each of the four broad industrial categories: cultivators, agricultural labourers, household industry workers, and "other" workers, in both rural and urban areas. For the country as a whole, the number of cultivators had increased by 48.9 per cent among females but by only 10.7 per cent among males. In rural areas, the decadal increase in male agricultural workers was almost three times that of male cultivators, but among women the decadal increase in cultivators was significantly higher than that of agricultural labourers. Also in the rural areas, the percentage increase in main workers engaged

in household-based industries was considerably higher among females (40.8 per cent) compared with males (18.0 per cent). Further, the decadal increase in both male and female main workers was much higher in the urban than in the rural areas (table 58).

The percentage distribution of main workers by three broad sectors, primary, secondary and tertiary, in 1981 and 1991 is shown in table 59. It will be noted that in 1981 as well as in 1991 a larger proportion among female than male main workers were employed in the primary sector, which comprises the two major sectors of agriculture and allied industries, and mining and quarrying. Consequently, a larger proportion among males than among females were employed in the secondary (manufacturing and construction) as well as in the tertiary (trade and commerce; transport and communications; other services) sectors. While there was hardly any change in the percentage distribution of female workers by the three broad groups in the rural areas between 1981 and 1991, in the urban areas there was a reduction in the proportion of female workers engaged in the secondary sector and an increase in their proportion in the tertiary sector during the same period.

Available data (not shown in table 59) also indicate that between 1981 and 1991, the proportion of female workers in the primary sector

Table 58. Percentage increase in the number of main workers by broad industrial category, sex and residence: 1981-1991

Residence	Sex	Percentage increase, 1981-1991				
		All main workers	Cultivators	Agricultural labourers	Household industry workers	Other
India	Both sexes	26.12	16.92	33.01	33.90	32.19
	Male	21.51	10.74	30.12	29.41	29.70
	Female	44.24	48.85	37.85	46.13	52.67
Urban	Both sexes	37.98	35.06	52.49	56.83	36.00
	Male	34.74	28.07	55.41	55.70	33.00
	Female	62.41	94.04	46.29	60.27	64.52
Rural	Both sexes	23.03	16.44	31.99	24.30	26.93
	Male	17.57	10.26	28.66	17.96	24.96
	Female	41.78	48.08	37.47	40.83	40.41

Source: Office of the Registrar General, India, *Census of India, 1991, Series I,* Paper No. 3 of 1991.

Table 59. Percentage distribution of main workers by primary, secondary and tertiary sectors, sex and residence: censuses of 1981 and 1991

Residence	Sex	1981 census				1991 census			
		Primary sector	Secondary sector	Tertiary sector	All sectors	Primary sector	Secondary sector	Tertiary sector	All sectors
India	Both sexes	69.41	12.96	17.63	100.00	67.37	12.13	20.50	100.00
	Male	66.28	13.96	19.76	100.00	63.37	13.30	23.32	100.00
	Female	81.61	9.04	9.35	100.00	81.09	8.07	10.84	100.00
Urban	Both sexes	14.04	33.79	52.17	100.00	14.52	30.27	55.21	100.00
	Male	12.77	34.52	52.71	100.00	13.26	31.06	55.68	100.00
	Female	23.74	28.13	48.13	100.00	22.94	24.97	52.09	100.00
Rural	Both sexes	83.86	7.52	8.62	100.00	82.75	6.84	10.41	100.00
	Male	82.18	7.86	9.96	100.00	80.36	7.29	12.35	100.00
	Female	89.45	6.44	4.11	100.00	89.80	5.54	4.66	100.00

Source: Office of the Registrar General, India, *Census of India, 1991, Series I: Final Population Totals,* Paper No. 2 of 1992.

Notes: The primary sector comprises agriculture and allied industries, and mining and quarrying.
The secondary sector comprises manufacturing, processing, servicing, repair, and construction.
The tertiary sector comprises trade and commerce, transport, storage and communications; and other services.

increased in all states excepting Kerala, Tamil Nadu, Maharashtra and West Bengal; the proportion of female workers employed in the secondary sector declined everywhere except in Kerala and West Bengal, while the proportion in the tertiary sector increased in all states but Rajasthan and West Bengal.

5. Employment patterns

In addition to the population census, there are two other important sources of data on employment. The National Sample Survey Organization has been carrying out surveys of employment and unemployment quinquennially since 1972/73. The Ministry of Labour conducts an Annual Survey of Industries and also collects data under the Employment Market Information Programme in respect of the organized sector of the economy. Data from these two sources are used to describe the employment patterns in the country.

(a) Growth rates

The average annual growth rates of employment (usual principal and subsidiary status) by sex and residence for the period 1972/73 to 1987/88 are shown in table 60. It will be noted that until 1983, female employment had been growing at a slightly higher rate than

Table 60. Annual growth rates of employment by sex: 1972/73 to 1987/88

(Percentage)

Period	Both sexes	Male	Female
1972/73-1977/78	2.82	2.61	3.23
1977/78-1983	2.22	2.15	2.36
1983-1987/88	1.55	1.81	1.04
1972/73-1987/88	2.21	2.19	2.24

Source: Planning Commission, *Employment: Past Trends and Prospects for 1990s* (New Delhi, 1990).

Note: Based on National Sample Survey data.

male employment, and that during the period 1983-1987/88, the rate of growth of male employment was slightly higher than that of female employment. During the entire period 1972/73 to 1977/78 the employment growth rate averaged 2.24 per cent per annum for males and 2.19 per cent for females.

Although overall employment has been growing at a slow rate in recent times, employment of the educated grew at a relatively high rate during the 10-year period 1977/78-1987/88, averaging 7.3 per cent per annum for males and 9.7 per cent for females. During the five-year period 1983-1988, the growth rate of employment of educated females averaged 11.7

per cent, compared with 7.5 per cent for males (table 61).

casual wage employees. It will also be noted that the overall trend during the 10-year period 1977/78 to 1987/88 appears to have been an increase in the proportion of women in paid employment, especially on a casual basis.

Table 61. Average annual growth rates of employment of educated persons by sex: 1977/78 to 1987/88

Period	Both sexes	Male	Female
1977/78-1983	7.2	7.2	8.1
1983-1987/88	7.8	7.5	11.7
1977/78-1987/88	7.5	7.3	9.7

Source: Planning Commission, *Employment: Past Trends and Prospects for 1990s* (New Delhi, 1990).

(b) Type of employment

The percentage distribution of workers by type of employment (self-employment, salaried regular employment, or casual wage employment) is given in table 62. It will be noted that in rural areas, most workers, among both males and females, are self-employed; in 1987/88 nearly 58 per cent of male and 55 per cent of female workers were in self-employment, while another 32 per cent of male and 40 per cent of female workers were casual wage employees. In the urban areas, however, the pattern is different, with an almost equal proportion of the workers, both male and female, being self-employed or in salaried regular employment. Among the 1987/88 urban salaried female employees, 27 per cent were

(c) Organized sector employment

It is estimated that about 10 per cent of total employment in the country is provided by the organized sector. Data from the Ministry of Labour indicate that women's employment in the organized sector has increased steadily and significantly in absolute as well as relative terms for over two decades. In 1970, less than 1.9 million, or about 11 per cent of the 17.04 million persons employed in the organized sector, were women, but 23 years later, in 1993, there were slightly over 4 million women employed in the organized sector, constituting 14.8 per cent of all workers in that sector (table 63).

Although the number of women employed in the organized sector as a whole had more than doubled from 1.89 million in 1970 to 4.02 million in 1993, this increase has been more marked in the public sector, where the number of women employees increased more than threefold from 0.81 million to 2.47 million during the 23-year period. Consequently, the number of women employed in the public sector as a proportion of all women employed in the entire organized sector increased from 42.9 per cent in 1970 to 61.4 per cent in 1993. Further,

Table 62. Percentage distribution of workers by type of employment and urban/rural area: 1977/78 to 1987/88

Employment type	Year	Urban			Rural		
		Both sexes	Male	Female	Both sexes	Male	Female
Self-employment	1977/78	40.3	39.9	42.2	60.4	62.2	56.3
	1983	39.7	40.2	37.3	57.8	59.5	54.1
	1987/88	40.5	41.0	38.6	56.7	57.5	55.1
Salaried regular	1977/78	44.2	47.2	30.8	8.6	10.9	3.7
employment	1983	42.2	44.5	31.8	8.5	10.6	3.7
	1987/88	42.7	44.4	34.7	8.6	10.4	4.7
Casual wage	1977/78	15.5	12.9	27.0	31.0	26.9	40.0
employment	1983	18.1	15.3	30.9	33.7	29.9	42.2
	1987/88	16.8	14.6	26.7	34.7	32.1	40.2

Source: National Sample Survey Organization, cited in Planning Commission, *Eighth Five-year Plan,* vol. 1.

Table 63. Employment in the organized sector by subsector and sex: 1970-1993

(Millions)

Year	Public sector				Private sector				Total organized sector			
	Both sexes	Male	Female	Percentage female	Both sexes	Male	Female	Percentage female	Both sexes	Male	Female	Percentage female
1970	10.35	9.54	0.81	7.8	6.69	5.61	1.08	16.1	17.04	15.15	1.89	11.1
1971	10.73	9.87	0.86	8.0	6.76	5.68	1.08	16.0	17.49	15.55	1.94	11.1
1975	12.87	11.74	1.13	8.8	6.80	5.70	1.10	16.2	19.67	17.44	2.23	11.3
1980	15.08	13.63	1.45	9.6	7.22	5.97	1.25	17.3	22.30	19.60	2.70	12.1
1981	15.47	13.98	1.49	9.6	7.39	6.10	1.29	17.5	22.86	20.08	2.78	12.2
1985	17.27	15.41	1.86	10.8	7.31	6.01	1.30	17.8	24.58	21.42	3.16	12.9
1990	18.77	16.52	2.25	12.0	7.58	6.19	1.39	18.3	26.35	22.71	3.64	13.8
1991	19.05	16.71	2.34	12.3	7.67	6.24	1.43	18.6	26.72	22.95	3.77	14.1
1993	19.31	16.84	2.47	12.8	7.85	6.30	1.55	19.7	27.16	23.14	4.02	14.8

Source: Ministry of Labour, Government of India.

women as a proportion of all employees increased from 7.8 to 12.8 per cent in the public sector and from 16.1 to 19.7 per cent in the private sector during the same 23-year period, indicating that in both subsectors, the employment growth rate has been higher for females than for males.

The distribution of organized sector employees by type of establishment and by gender in 1980 and 1990 is given in table 64.

It is evident from table 64 that within the public sector, the largest number of workers are employed by the state governments, followed by the central government and the local bodies. Of the 18.77 million workers employed in the public sector in 1990, as many as 9.63 million, or 51.3 per cent, were employees of state governments (including state government quasi), and the proportion was 53.8 per cent for females and about 51 per cent for males. Although the state governments employ the

Table 64. Distribution of employees in the organized sector by type of establishment and sex: 1980 and 1990

(Millions)

Subsector/ establishment	1980				1990			
	Both sexes	Male	Female	Percentage female	Both sexes	Male	Female	Percentage female
Public sector	**15.08**	**13.63**	**1.45**	**9.6**	**18.77**	**16.52**	**2.25**	**12.0**
Central government	3.18	3.05	0.13	4.1	3.40	3.19	0.21	6.2
State government	5.48	4.87	0.61	11.1	6.98	5.95	1.03	14.8
Central government (Quasi)	2.60	2.42	0.18	6.9	3.52	3.23	0.29	8.2
State government (Quasi)	1.74	1.63	0.11	6.3	2.65	2.47	0.18	6.8
Local bodies	2.08	1.66	0.42	20.2	2.22	1.68	0.54	24.3
Private sector	**7.22**	**5.97**	**1.25**	**17.3**	**7.58**	**6.19**	**1.39**	**18.3**
Large establishments	6.48	5.36	1.12	17.3	6.71	5.50	1.21	18.0
Small establishments	0.74	0.61	0.13	17.6	0.87	0.69	0.18	20.7
Total organized sector	**22.30**	**19.60**	**2.70**	**12.1**	**26.35**	**22.71**	**3.64**	**13.8**

Source: Ministry of Labour, Government of India.

70

largest number of women, the proportionate share of women in total employment is highest (24.3 per cent) in local bodies. In the private sector, the vast majority of men (88.9 per cent) as well as women (87.1 per cent) employees are engaged by the large establishments.

(d) Employment in the informal sector

Although official statistics do not provide a more accurate picture of women's employment levels and patterns, other data and estimates suggest that an increasing number of women find work and earn income in the informal sector, particularly in the urban areas. According to conservative estimates based on the 1981 census data, about 53 per cent of urban female workers were engaged in the informal sector, but estimates based on the 1983 National Sample Survey data showed this proportion to be 75 per cent. Several micro-studies have reported that female work participation rates are considerably higher in the informal than in the formal sector. For example, a 1988 study of two large and four medium-sized urban centres in different regions of the country revealed that the work participation rate for females aged 15 years and over was 49 per cent in the informal sector and only 31 per cent in the formal sector (National Institute of Urban Affairs, 1988).

Available studies also show that rural-to-urban migrants, especially the women among them, constitute a substantial proportion of urban informal sector workers. Owing to the sluggish growth of employment opportunities in the urban formal sector, the majority of migrants from rural areas are compelled to seek work in the informal sector. Several in-depth studies carried out in various cities have also shown conclusively that the vast majority, about 70 per cent, of women engaged in informal sector occupations were below the poverty line (Banerjee, 1985; Bapat, and Crook, 1988).

Several studies have also shown that within the informal sector, women workers are largely concentrated in the service and manufacturing subsectors. Initially, most migrant women take up employment as domestic servants but gradually move on to non-tradi-

tional employment when opportunities arise. In the manufacturing sector, the employment of women falls under three categories. First, a number of women tend to be engaged as casual wage earners in several establishments and processes using more traditional, labour-intensive technologies. A 1985 study showed that in those industries employing a high proportion of women, the capital/labour ratio as well as the output/worker ratio were well below the national averages (Banerjee, 1985). The second category comprises an increasing number of women working on a piece-rate basis (putting out system); enterprises contract out certain steps in the production process on a piece-rate basis to be completed in work-shops run by contractors or in the women's homes. The third category of women workers in the urban informal sector includes the self-employed working in a wide range of service and manufacturing occupations using simple technologies and limited resources. This category includes vendors, hawkers, petty traders, laundry servicers, rag pickers, cart pullers, caterers and food processors and all sorts of petty manufacturing (Bennett, 1992).

Besides lack of employment opportunities in the formal sector, several other factors have contributed to the increasing number of informal sector workers. In the first instance, the casual employment and piecework arrangements enable large registered establishments to circumvent legal and collective bargaining restrictions on retrenchments and to maintain flexibility in the size of their labour force. Even for small entrepreneurs, these arrangements provide a flexible way to hire workers when needed. Second, since the skills required are minimal and the supply of low-skill labour is increasing, it will be possible to substitute one worker for another without difficulty. Indeed, the possibility of the substitution of workers is an important factor contributing to the easy entry of women into new occupations in the informal sector.

The working conditions, in the case of wage employment, in the informal sector are often difficult, with hardly any security of employment or legal protection. Opportunities for skill development or technology upgrading to increase productivity are limited, and access to infrastructure facilities, credit, raw materials (at reasonable prices), markets, services and information is poor. Poverty, illiteracy and the lack of organization of women in the informal sector aggravate their vulnerability and exploitation by way of irregular, uncertain and low incomes. Technological change and mechanization in segments in which women are employed in large numbers often lead to their displacement. Apprehension has therefore been expressed as to the likely impact on employment of the structural adjustment programmes and the new economic policies, more specifically in those unorganized sectors in which the bulk of women are employed.

(e) Wage differentials

Data from various surveys and studies indicate that there are significant differences in the average earnings of male and female workers in both the rural and urban areas. Such differentials could partly be explained by the fact that a greater proportion among female workers compared with male workers are concentrated in unskilled, low-productivity and low-status jobs. But investigations have also shown that even when men and women are at the same skill level and perform identical duties, earnings of females are significantly lower than those of males.

In regard to gender wage differentials in the agricultural sector, a 1988 study based on data from the Rural Labour Enquiries of 1964/65 and 1974/75 has shown conclusively that women workers belonging to agricultural labour households, irrespective of their caste or region, received significantly lower wages than their male counterparts in various agricultural operations. However, the study also reported a narrowing in gender differentials in wages between 1964/65 and 1974/75 (Krishnamurty, 1988).

The prevalence of gender differentials in wages is also confirmed by another independent study, also undertaken in 1988, based on data published by the Ministry of Agriculture, Government of India (Jose, 1988). According to this study, while female wages in agriculture were lower than the male wages in all the 16 large states included in the analysis, there was considerable variation across the states with regard to the extent of this disparity. For instance, in 1984/85 the ratio of female wage to male wage was less than 80 per cent in 10 of the 16 states, and less than 65 per cent in three states: Tamil Nadu (57.2 per cent), Rajasthan (60.4 per cent) and Maharashtra (64.2 per cent). This ratio exceeded 80 per cent in Assam, Bihar, Karnataka, Madhya Pradesh, Punjab and Himachal Pradesh. The study also found that while there was a distinct tendency for the gender disparity in wages to narrow down between 1970/71 and 1984/85 in most of the 16 states, in some states, such as Maharashtra, Tamil Nadu and Rajasthan, the disparity was more or less maintained throughout the 14-year period (table 65).

6. Unemployment levels

A striking feature of employment for women in recent decades has been their relatively high unemployment rates. Available estimates indicate that the incidence of female unemployment is higher in the urban than in the rural areas. For instance, in 1990/91, the unemployment rate based on usual status (adjusted) was 4.7 per cent for urban women as against only 0.3 per cent for rural women. Estimates based on current weekly status also give a much higher female unemployment rate in urban areas (5.3 per cent) than in rural (2.1 per cent) areas (table 66). Available data also indicate that the number of women on the live register of the employment exchanges in the country had increased by 2.4 lakhs from 78.50 lakhs as at the end of 1993 to 80.90 lakhs at the end of 1984.

Several factors have contributed to the relatively high unemployment rates for women, particularly in the urban areas. An important factor is the lack of appropriate skills; women also tend to become easily displaced by new technologies and are either pushed out or pushed down when job requirements call for skilled and trained persons. Ironically, another important factor contributing to women's unemployment is the entry into the labour market of educated women in increasing numbers,

Table 65. Agricultural wage rates by state and sex: 1970/71 and 1984/85

| Region/state | Agricultural wage rates (rupees per day) | | | | Ratio of female/male rates | |
| | 1970/71 | | 1984/85 | | 1970/71 | 1984/85 |
	Male	Female	Male	Female		
Eastern						
Assam	3.96	3.14	12.87	10.65	79.3	82.7
Bihar	2.64	2.15	9.88	9.16	81.4	92.7
Orissa	2.19	1.48	8.42	5.99	67.6	71.1
West Bengal	4.04	2.37	10.59	8.39	58.7	79.2
Southern						
Andhra Pradesh	2.70	1.96	10.41	7.64	72.6	73.4
Karnataka	2.45	1.68	7.31	5.93	68.6	81.1
Kerala	4.61	2.81	16.86	12.34	61.0	73.2
Tamil Nadu	2.53	1.42	8.83	5.05	56.1	57.2
Central						
Madhya Pradesh	2.15	1.54	8.53	7.11	71.6	83.4
Uttar Pradesh	2.72	1.92	10.54	8.24	70.6	78.2
Western						
Gujarat	3.07	2.33	12.58	9.80	75.8	77.9
Maharashtra	2.84	1.84	9.46	6.07	64.8	64.2
Northern						
Haryana	6.64	3.96	19.35	14.99	59.6	77.5
Punjab	6.39	4.08	18.13	14.91	63.8	82.2
Himachal Pradesh	4.11	3.48	12.55	11.25	84.7	89.6
Rajasthan	3.69	1.88	12.63	7.63	50.9	60.4

Source: A.V. Jose, "Agricultural wages in India", *Economic and Political Weekly,* 25 June 1988.

Table 66. Unemployment rates by sex and residence: 1972/73 to 1990/91

(Per thousand persons in the labour force)

| Year | Residence | Male | | | Female | | |
		Usual status	Usual status adjusted	Current weekly status	Usual status	Usual status adjusted	Current weekly status
1972/73	Urban	n.a.	48	60	n.a.	60	92
	Rural	n.a.	12	30	n.a.	5	55
1977/78	Urban	65	54	71	178	124	109
	Rural	22	13	36	55	20	41
1983	Urban	59	51	67	69	49	75
	Rural	21	14	37	14	7	43
1987/88	Urban	61	52	66	85	62	92
	Rural	28	18	42	35	24	44
1989/90	Urban	44	39	45	39	27	40
	Rural	16	13	26	8	6	21
1990/91	Urban	45	45	51	54	47	53
	Rural	13	11	22	4	3	21

Source: Sarvekshana, July-September 1992, cited in Government of India, *Fourth World Conference on Women, Beijing, 1995: Country Report.*

n.a. = not available.

both because more and more women are graduating from universities and because there is now a trend for educated women to seek a career. This trend is reflected in the increase in the number of women with matriculation and higher qualifications on the live registers of employment exchanges (table 67).

It will be noted from table 67 that the number of women with various levels of educational attainment on the live register of employment exchanges increased tremendously between 1970 and 1990. This increase was almost fourteenfold in the case of women applicants who had completed their secondary education (matriculation), and almost twentyfold in respect of women with higher secondary education and for those with university degrees. The number of women applicants with postgraduate qualifications increased nineteenfold during this period. These increases are also reflected in the increases in the proportionate share of women among total registrants with various levels of educational attainments. The

relative share of women among all registrants increased from 16.6 per cent in 1970 to 20.7 per cent in 1990 in the case of those with secondary education; from 10.7 to 20.1 per cent for those with higher secondary education; from 16.3 to 25.4 per cent for university graduates; and from 25.4 to 35.6 per cent for those with postgraduate qualifications.

F. WOMEN IN PUBLIC LIFE

1. Women in politics

(a) Background

For a long time in the past, Indian women had played an important and dynamic role in the political life of their country. In particular, the freedom movement for India's independence from British colonial rule, spearheaded by the Indian National Congress since 1885, provided a tremendous opportunity for Indian women to be involved in a mass and popular protest movement. In 1900, the first women

Table 67. Number of applicants with matriculation and higher educational qualifications on the live register of employment exchanges, by sex: 1970-1990

| Educational level | Year | Number of applicants on the live register | | | |
		Both sexes	Male	Female	Percentage female
Matriculate	1970	1 101 194	918 956	182 238	16.55
	1975	2 641 213	2 235 980	405 233	15.34
	1980	4 568 225	3 800 337	767 888	16.81
	1985	8 045 287	6 409 768	1 635 519	20.33
	1990	12 327 664	9 778 898	2 548 766	20.68
Higher secondary	1970	443 884	396 373	47 511	10.70
	1975	1 228 147	1 082 011	146 136	11.90
	1980	2 070 935	1 750 972	319 963	15.45
	1985	3 530 440	2 906 537	623 903	17.67
	1990	5 156 369	4 121 018	1 035 351	20.08
Graduate	1970	245 076	205 032	40 044	16.34
	1975	858 674	717 690	140 984	16.42
	1980	1 389 771	1 107 815	281 956	20.29
	1985	2 128 073	1 641 092	486 981	22.88
	1990	3 200 176	2 385 094	815 082	25.47
Postgraduate	1970	31 462	23 457	8 005	25.44
	1975	77 192	56 854	20 338	26.35
	1980	134 614	98 380	36 234	26.92
	1985	271 716	223 627	48 089	17.70
	1990	422 627	272 059	150 568	35.63

Source: Ministry of Labour, Government of India.

delegates attended a session of the Indian National Congress held in Calcutta and spoke from a political platform. Since then Indian women from all age groups, classes, castes and religions emerged in their thousands in response to the call of Mahathma Gandhi to join the freedom struggle. Women became more visible in the political arena in 1925 when Sarojini Naidu was elected the first woman President of the Indian National Congress. During the 1942 "Quit India" movement, when most of the male leaders were arrested and jailed, women assumed leadership roles in the movement.

In the post-independence period, women have continued to speak out on all issues. The women's movements and women's organizations have advocated policy changes and constitutional amendments, reflecting and articulating the experiences and aspirations of the country's women. Prior to independence, women had only limited adult franchise, but after independence equal voting rights were guaranteed under the Constitution; consequently, women have been participating in the political process as voters, as candidates contesting election, and in deliberations in state assemblies and the National Parliament, and have also held public office at various levels. Most national-level and regional political parties have a women's wing, as for example, the National Federation of Indian Women of the Communist Party of India, the Mahila Dakshata Samiti of the Janata Party, and the Mahila Congress of the Congress (I). India can also boast of having had a democratically elected woman Prime Minister and democratically elected chief ministers in some states.

Although women have been in the forefront in political activities, their presence has not been felt strongly in structured decision-making and institutions. Over the years, only a very few women have been situated at political levels that are significant and effective for exercising power and authority. As succinctly stated in the National Perspective Plan for Women 1988-2000, "women are still left on the periphery of the political process, and political participation remains elusive to most of them in spite of their voting and election and also capture of some seats of power and influence". Women are increasingly involving themselves in matters which affect their lives directly and indirectly, mainly through non-governmental organizations. Some political analysts consider this as an alternative stream of quasi-political participation by women.

(b) Women as voters

In India, women account for nearly half of all persons legally entitled to exercise their franchise or right of voting at public elections. Yet, it would appear that Indian women have been exercising this right to a lesser extent than their male counterparts. The relatively poor participation of women vis-à-vis men in the electoral process is evidenced by available gender data on the number of persons registered as electors for casting votes as well as the proportions of electors actually voting at successive elections to the House of People (Lok Sabha) of the National Parliament shown in table 68.

It is evident from table 68 that the number of eligible females registering themselves as electors increased more than threefold from 77.9 million at the first elections held in 1952 to 245.6 million at the tenth elections held in 1991. This rate of increase was somewhat higher than the 2.7 fold increase in the number of eligible males registered during the same period: from 95.3 million to 261.8 million. Consequently, the proportion of females in the total number of electors increased from 45 per cent in 1952 to 48.4 per cent in 1991. Yet in 1991, the number of male electors exceeded that of female electors by 16.2 million.

It is clear from table 68 that not only are a smaller proportion of women than men registered as electors, but also the proportion of registered electors who actually vote at various national elections is lower among females than among males. For instance, at the 1991 elections, only 49.5 per cent of all registered female electors went to the polls, the corresponding proportion for males being 61.6 per cent, or 12.1 percentage points higher than

Table 68. Number of registered electors and voters at various elections to the House of People (Lok Sabha) of the Indian Parliament, by sex: election years of 1952 to 1991

Election year	Electors registered for casting vote at elections (millions)				Electors actually voted at elections					
					Number (millions)			Percentage of registered electors		
	Both sexes	Male	Female	Percent- age female	Both sexes	Male	Female	Both sexes	Male	Female
1952	173.2	95.3	77.9	45.0	80.7	51.0	29.7	46.6	53.5	38.1
1957	193.6	102.2	91.4	47.2	91.3	55.9	35.4	47.2	54.7	38.7
1962	216.3	113.9	102.4	47.3	118.5	70.7	47.8	54.8	62.1	46.7
1967	250.6	130.4	120.2	48.0	152.7	86.4	66.3	60.9	66.2	55.2
1971	274.1	143.5	130.6	47.6	151.6	87.4	64.2	55.3	60.9	49.2
1977	321.2	167.0	154.2	48.0	194.3	109.6	84.7	60.4	65.6	54.9
1980	355.6	185.2	170.4	47.9	202.4	115.1	87.3	56.9	62.1	51.2
1984	379.5	196.7	182.8	48.2	241.2	134.1	107.1	63.6	68.2	58.6
1989	498.9	262.0	236.9	47.5	308.9	173.2	135.7	61.9	66.1	57.3
1991	507.4	261.8	245.6	48.4	282.9	161.3	121.6	55.7	61.6	49.5

Sources: Data up to 1984 from *Women in India: A Statistical Profile* (Department of Women and Child Development, Government of India, 1988); data for 1991 from *Report of the Tenth General Election to the House of People of India, 1991* (Election Commission of India).

for females. It will also be noted from table 68 that the proportion of registered electors, among both males and females, actually exercising their voting rights had fluctuated between 1952 and 1991. For women, this proportion had shown a remarkable increase from 38.1 per cent in 1952 to 55.2 per cent in 1967, thereafter declining to 49.2 per cent in 1977 and then rising to 54.9 per cent in 1977, falling again to 51.2 per cent in 1980, increasing to 58.6 per cent in 1984 and declining to 51.3 per cent in 1989 and further to 49.5 in 1991. A similar trend is noticeable in the case of male electors.

The participation of women in the electoral process is dependent on several factors, such as their mobilization by political parties; general awareness among the community, especially among the women themselves, of the importance of voting; and socio-cultural norms relating to women's participation in political activities. Generally, serious efforts have so far not been made by any political party to mobilize women as a political constituency. Available information (table 69) also indicates that the extent of women's participation in the electoral process also varies from state to state, depending on the level of educational attainment of women. For instance, data relating to the 1991

elections to seven state legislative assemblies show that the proportionate share of females in the total number of registered electors varies from 45 per cent in Uttar Pradesh, an educationally backward state, to about 51 per cent in Kerala, where female literacy is very high. Similarly, the proportion of female registered electors who actually went to the polls in the 1991 state assembly elections was also lowest in Uttar Pradesh (44.3 per cent) but was considerably higher in Kerala (73.3 per cent), Assam (73.9 per cent) and West Bengal (76.0 per cent).

(c) Women as candidates

The participation of women in the electoral process as candidates is very much poorer than their participation as registered electors and actual voters. According to data available from the Election Commission of India, less than 4 per cent of all candidates standing for election to the Lok Sabha in various years have been women, although this proportion had increased more or less steadily from 2.7 per cent at the first elections in 1952 to 3.7 per cent at the tenth elections held in 1991. There is a reluctance on the part of political parties to field women candidates. Besides, the high cost of election campaigns also deters women from coming forward as candidates. Available

Table 69. Electors and voters by sex at the general elections to state assemblies in selected states: 1991

| State | Electors registered for casting vote (millions) | | | | Electors actually voted at elections | | | | | |
| | | | | | Number (millions) | | | As percentage of registered electors | | |
	Both sexes	Male	Female	Percent-age female	Both sexes	Male	Female	Both sexes	Male	Female
Assam	11.89	6.37	5.52	46.4	8.88	4.80	4.08	74.7	75.4	73.9
Haryana	9.72	5.25	4.47	46.0	6.41	3.60	2.81	65.9	68.6	62.9
Kerala	19.66	9.72	9.94	50.6	14.44	7.15	7.29	73.4	73.6	73.3
Tamil Nadu	39.92	20.22	19.74	49.4	25.43	13.28	12.15	63.7	65.7	61.6
Uttar Bengal	79.31	43.59	35.72	45.0	39.11	23.28	15.83	49.3	53.4	44.3
West Bengal	41.36	22.12	19.26	46.6	31.78	17.15	14.63	76.8	77.5	76.0
Pondicheri	0.60	0.31	0.29	48.3	0.41	0.21	0.20	68.3	67.7	69.0
Total	202.48	107.58	94.90	46.9	126.46	69.47	56.99	62.4	64.6	60.0

Source: Statistical Reports, Election Commission of India, cited in Government of India, *Fourth World Conference on Women, Beijing, 1995: Country Report.*

data indicate that the chances of women being elected are very low; while at the elections held until 1967, about 37-60 per cent of women candidates were elected to the Lok Sabha, this proportion has declined steadily, from 25.6 in 1984 to 11.1 per cent in 1991 (table 70).

The participation of women in the elections as candidates also varies from state to state. Data relating to the 1991 elections to the legislative assemblies of six states and one union territory show that the relative share of women in the total number of candidates nominated to contest these elections varied from a low of 2.2 per cent in Haryana and 2.4 per cent in Pondicheri to 3.4 per cent in Tamil Nadu and 3.5 per cent in West Bengal. Similarly, the proportion of women in the total number of candidates who finally contested the elections was lowest (2.2 per cent) in Haryana and highest in Tamil Nadu (3.6 per cent) and West Bengal (3.9 per cent). In all seven states combined, women constituted 2.9 per cent of all candidates nominated and 3.1

Table 70. Contestants and successful candidates in Lok Sabha elections, by sex: 1952-1991

| Election year | Number of seats contested | Number of contestants | | | | Number elected | | Elected as percentage of respective contestants | |
		Both sexes	Male	Female	Percent-age female	Male	Female	Male	Female
1952	486	1 874	1 823	51	2.7	467	19	25.6	37.3
1957	494	1 518	1 473	45	3.0	467	27	31.7	60.0
1962	494	1 985	1 915	70	3.5	459	35	24.0	50.0
1967	520	2 369	2 302	67	2.8	490	30	21.3	44.8
1971	520	2 784	2 698	86	3.1	497	21	18.4	24.4
1977	542	2 439	2 369	70	2.9	523	19	22.1	27.1
1980	542	4 620	4 478	142	3.1	514	28	11.5	19.7
1984	542	5 574	5 410	164	2.9	500	42	9.2	25.6
1989	529	6 160	5 962	198	3.2	502	27	8.4	13.6
1991	521	8 699	8 374	325	3.7	485	36	5.8	11.1

Source: Election Commission of India, reports for various years.

per cent of all candidates who contested the legislative assembly elections (table 71).

(d) Women as legislators

Despite the fact that women constitute almost 50 per cent of India's population, their representation in the two houses of the National Parliament has been very low. In the Lok Sabha, which is the highest representative body in the country, women have all along constituted less than 8 per cent of the total membership. The relative share of women in Lok Sabha membership increased from 2.9 per cent in the period 1952-1957 to 6.1 per cent in the period 1962-1967, but thereafter it has been fluctuating, and in 1991 only 39, or 7.3 per cent, of all Lok Sabha members were women (table 72). Thus, despite the constitutional and legal guarantees and a galaxy of outstanding women leaders, including a Prime Minister for 16 years, Indian women continue to be grossly underrepresented in the highest legislative chamber of the country.

However, in the Upper House, Rajya Sabha, of the Indian Parliament, women enjoyed greater representation. According to data from the Election Commission, the relative share of women in total membership in the Rajya Sabha had increased from 7.3 per cent in 1952 to around 10 per cent between 1977 and 1990. In 1991, women constituted about 15.5 per cent of the total members in the Rajya Sabha

(table 73). The relatively higher representative of women in the Rajya Sabha is due to the fact that membership of this chamber is by indirect election and nomination.

Some studies relating to parliamentary participation have reported that, generally, women members participate more actively in "women's issues", particularly health, welfare, violence against women, dowry, and violation

Table 72. Women's representation in the Lok Sabha (Lower House): 1952-1957 to 1991

Term of Lok Sabha	Membership of Lok Sabha		
	Total	Women	Percent-age women
1952-1957	489	14	2.9
1957-1962	494	18	3.6
1962-1967	494	30	6.1
1967-1971	520	31	6.0
1971-1977	520	20	3.8
1977-1980	542	19	3.5
1980-1984[a]	429	28	6.5
1984-1989	542	42	7.7
1989-1991[a]	523	23	4.4
1991	536	39	7.3

Source: Election Commission of India, cited in Government of India, *Fourth World Conference on Women, Beijing, 1995: Country Report.*

[a] Elections were not held in 1980 in 12 constituencies in Assam and in Meghalaya: in 1989, elections were not held in Jammu and Kashmir.

Table 71. Candidates nominated for and candidates contesting elections to the legislative assemblies of six states and one union territory: 1991

State/union territory	Total seats	Number of candidates nominated				Number of candidates contested			
		Both sexes	Male	Female	Percent-age female	Both sexes	Male	Female	Percent-age female
Assam	126	2 073	2 012	61	2.9	1 657	1 607	50	3.0
Haryana	90	4 062	3 973	89	2.2	1 885	1 844	41	2.2
Kerala	140	1 336	1 297	39	2.9	809	783	26	3.2
Tamil Nadu	234	4 699	4 540	159	3.4	2 843	2 741	102	3.6
Uttar Pradesh	425	14 882	14 445	437	2.9	7 851	7 622	229	2.9
West Bengal	294	2 287	2 207	80	3.5	1 903	1 829	74	3.9
Pondicheri	30	335	327	8	2.4	208	202	6	2.9
Total	1 339	29 674	28 801	873	2.9	17 156	16 628	528	3.1

Source: Statistical Reports, Election Commission of India, cited in Government of India, *Fourth World Conference on Women, Beijing, 1995: Country Report.*

Table 73. Women's representation in the Rajya Sabha (Upper House) of the Indian Parliament: 1952-1991

Year	Membership of Rajya Sabha		
	Total	Women	Percentage women
1952	219	16	7.3
1957	237	18	7.6
1962	238	18	7.6
1967	240	20	8.3
1971	243	17	7.0
1977	244	25	10.2
1980	244	24	9.8
1985	244	28	11.5
1990	245	24	9.8
1991	245	38	15.5

Source: Election Commission of India, *cited in Government of India, Fourth World Conference on Women, Beijing, 1995: Country Report.*

of human rights, and that their participation is relatively limited in issues concerning defence, finance etc.

A recent analysis indicates that there has, by and large, been no improvement in women's representation in selected state legislature. In fact, in most of the 10 states included in the analysis, the relative share of women in the total membership of the state legislative assembles has declined over the years since the 1950s. Data for the early 1990s show that this share had varied from a low of 2.8 per

cent in Uttar Pradesh to a high of 6.1 per cent in West Bengal (table 74).

In 1995, there was one woman senior minister and six state ministers in a Cabinet of 74 at the national level. Over the years, women ministers were entrusted with welfare-oriented portfolios such as women and development, culture and youth, and were rarely in charge of such subjects as finance, defence, foreign relations or science and technology, although several women have demonstrated their capability in these areas.

As noted in the introductory section of this profile, a change of far-reaching consequence is the 73rd and 74th amendments to the Indian Constitution, which give constitutional recognition to a third tier of elected representatives below the centre and the states, that is, panchayats in rural areas and municipal bodies in urban areas. These amendments vest the local governments with financial and administrative powers and give them developmental responsibilities which now find a place in the Eleventh Schedule of the Constitution. Under the terms of these amendments, one third of the seats in these various elected local bodies are to be reserved for women, and one third of the chairpersons of panchayats at all levels are to be women. This far-reaching step has undoubtedly paved the way for greater participation of women in public affairs at the grass-roots level and helped to provide a wide

Table 74. Representation of women in state legislative assemblies

States	Membership of state legislature				Membership of state legistature			
	Year	Total	Women	Percentage women	Year	Total	Women	Percentage women
Andhra Pradesh	1957	252	11	4.4	1994	294	9	3.1
Karnataka	1957	179	18	10.1	1994	224	7	3.1
Kerala	1957	127	6	4.7	1991	140	8	5.7
Madhya Pradesh	1957	218	26	11.9	1993	320	12	3.8
Punjab	1957	101	5	5.0	1992	117	6	5.1
Rajasthan	1957	136	9	6.6	1993	200	9	4.5
Tripura	1967	30	0	0.0	1992	60	2	3.3
Uttar Pradesh	1957	341	24	7.0	1993	425	12	2.8
West Bengal	1957	195	11	5.6	1991	294	18	6.1
Delhi	1972	56	3	5.4	1993	70	3	4.3

Source: Institute of Social Sciences, *A status Report on Participation of Women in Panchayati Raj* (New Delhi, 1995).

base for the development of women leaders. The reservation of seats and removal of co-option had enabled women to contest elections, thus putting an end to the nomination of favourites by male political bosses.

The success of the reservation system is attested to by the results of the elections for various levels of panchayats held in several states. It will be noted from table 75 that, by and large, the reserved quotas have been filled and that women have gained more than the number of seats reserved for them in Karnataka and West Bengal. This overwhelming response is unprecedented in Indian history.

2. Women in public administration

As noted earlier in section E, "Women in economic life", the employment of women in the public sector (comprising central government, state governments and local governments) had been steadily increasing, from about 810 thousand in 1970 to 2.47 million in 1993. But in the two premier civil services, the Indian Administrative Service and the Indian Foreign Service, women continue to be very much underrepresented. Data for the 20-year period 1972-1992 indicate that within the Indian Administrative Service, although the number of females more than tripled from 115 in 1972 to 445 in 1992, women accounted for only about 9 per cent of the total cadre in this service in 1992. The representation of women in the Indian Foreign Service appears to be slightly

better, with about 11 per cent of positions in this service being occupied by women in 1992 (table 76).

The low proportion of women in the Indian Administrative Service and the Indian Foreign Service is due to the fact that until recent times not many women presented themselves as candidates for recruitment, which is through a centrally conducted competitive examination and limited to university graduates below 23 years of age. The low proportion and late entry of women into these services also mean that relatively few women are occupying positions at senior decision-making levels, such as heads of departments and secretaries of ministries, at the national and state levels. Since relatively few women enter the civil services, several efforts have been made to improve the situation. The Department of Personnel and Administrative Reforms of the Government of India has also provided, whenever possible, women officers on the selection boards for posts and services. At present, the chairperson of the Union Public Service Commission is a woman.

3. Women in the judiciary

In India, women are also very much underrepresented in the judiciary, particularly in the Supreme Court and high courts. Available data indicate that at present there is no woman serving as a judge of the Supreme Court, while of the 36 high court judges in

Table 75. Women in Panchayat Raj institutions

State	Year	Gram Panchayat (GP)				Panchayat Samitr (PS)				Zill Parichad (ZP)			
		Number of GPs	Membership			Number of PSs	Membership			Number of ZPs	Membership		
			Total	Women	Percentage women		Total	Women	Percentage women		Total	Women	Percentage women
Gujarat	1995	13 256	64 052	19 936	31.1	182	3 765	1 275	33.9	19	761	254	33.4
Haryana	1994	5 958	54 159	17 928	33.1	110	2 418	807	33.4	16	303	101	33.3
Karnataka	1993	5 641	80 627	37 689	46.7	175	3 340	1 343	40.2	20	919	335	36.5
Kerala	1995	990	10 700	3 878	36.2	152	1 543	565	36.6	14	300	104	34.7
Madhya Pradesh	1994	30 922	443 429	147 809	33.3	459	24 024	8 222	34.2	45	942	315	33.4
Punjab	1993	11 596	60 584	8 776	14.5	136	9 097	2 991	32.9	14	273	89	32.6
Rajasthan	1995	9 189	103 712	36 722	35.4	237	5 231	1 738	33.2	31	997	331	33.2
Tripura	1994	525	5 427	1 809	33.3	16	196	67	34.2	3	70	24	34.3
West Bengal	1993	3 223	61 011	21 489	35.2	328	9 453	3 182	33.7	16	656	224	34.1

Source: Institute of Social Sciences, cited in Government of India, *Fourth World Conference on Women, Beijing, 1995: Country Report.*

80

**Table 76. Women in the Indian Administrative Service and in the Indian Foreign Service:
1972-1992**

Year	Indian Administrative Service				Indian Foreign Service			
	Both sexes	Male	Female	Percent- age female	Both sexes	Male	Female	Percent- age female
1972	1 877	1 762	115	6.1	384	365	19	4.9
1975	2 286	2 124	162	7.1	338	308	30	8.9
1977	2 556	2 338	218	8.5	409	371	38	9.3
1982	n.a.	n.a.	n.a.	–	536	497	39	7.3
1985	4 284	3 973	311	7.3	535	485	50	9.3
1987	4 548	4 209	339	7.5	533	480	53	9.9
1992	4 981	4 536	445	8.9	523	464	59	11.3

Source: Department of Women and Child Development, Ministry of Human Resources Development, Government of India.

n.a. = not available.

1992, only 16, or 3.7 per cent, were women (table 77).

4. Women in the teaching profession

In India, some professions/occupations such as teaching have drawn more women than others. Data from the Department of Education indicate that during the past four decades there has been a progressive improvement in the number of female teachers at different levels of education. The ratio of female teachers per 100 male teachers increased from 20 in 1950/51 to 42 in 1993/94 at the primary level; from 18 to 52 in the middle schools; and from 19 to 50 at the higher secondary level. Available data also indicate that an increasing number of females have been recruited as teachers in colleges and universities and the ratio of female to male tea-

chers increased from 9 in 1950/51 to 28 in 1985/86 (table 78).

G. SPECIAL CONCERNS

1. Crimes against women

The physical vulnerability of women makes them victims of various crimes such as rape, kidnapping and abduction, torture, "dowry burning and deaths", molestation and eve-teasing. However, an accurate assessment of the extent of various crimes committed against women is hampered by a lack of comprehensive data and information. In India, as in most countries the world over, official data deal with crime *per se* rather than the more pervasive phenomenon of violence in its different facets. Further, police data on crimes are based on actual complaints, the lodging of which in turn depends

Table 77. Women in the judiciary: 1975-1992

Year	Judges in the Supreme Court			Judges in the High Courts		
	Total	Women	Percentage women	Total	Women	Percentage women
1975	13	–	–	299	1	0.3
1987	16	–	–	391	11	2.8
1989	26	1	3.8	387	12	3.1
1992	25	–	–	436	16	3.7

Source: Margaret Alva, "Role of women political leaders in community development: India" in ESCAP, *Women in Politics in Asia and the Pacific.*

Table 78. Number of female teachers per 100 male teachers at different levels of education:
1950/51 to 1993/94

Year	Female teachers per 100 male teachers in			
	Primary schools	Middle schools	Higher secondary schools	Colleges and universities
1950/51	20	18	19	9
1955/56	20	19	23	12
1960/61	21	32	27	14
1965/66	24	30	30	16
1970/71	27	38	33	18
1975/76	29	40	36	20
1980/81	33	42	38	24
1985/86	37	46	43	28
1990/91	41	50	46	n.a.
1991/92	42	49	45	n.a.
1992/93	41	47	49	n.a.
1993/94	42	52	50	n.a.

Source: Department of Education, Ministry of Human Resources Development, cited in Central Statistical Organization, *Women and Men in India, 1995* (New Delhi, Ministry of Planning, Government of India, 1995).

n.a. = not available.

on willingness on the part of the victims to report the offences, as well as on the sensitivity and inclination of the police to investigate and act on the complaints. Besides, in many cases female victims, particularly of psychological oppression, are not sufficiently aware of the implications of the crimes either to themselves or to the perpetrator in order to articulate them.

Although the incidence of domestic violence is considered to be fairly widespread in rural as well as urban areas, and women and girl children in many households are subject to discrimination, torture, beating and injury, accurate data on the magnitude of domestic violence against women are not available, as most cases go unreported. Available evidence also suggests an increase in marital violence and wife abuse which manifests itself in various forms, ranging from long hours of labour within and outside the household, denial of food, neglect of ailments, and verbal abuse to physical violence by the husband and sometimes other members of the family. There also appears to be a tendency to brand all marital violence as "dowry violence" or "dowry deaths", thereby glossing over the other causes of such violence.

It is, however, encouraging to note that the National Crime Records Bureau has started collecting more detailed information on various forms of crimes committed against women. The reporting of such crimes has also increased significantly over the years owing to greater awareness of the legal provisions of women's rights, as well as to the determined efforts on the part of women themselves and of the community to break the culture of silence surrounding atrocities against women. The media are also playing an important role by reporting several incidents and furnishing statistics on rape, molestation, incest, assault, dowry deaths etc.

Available data suggest an increasing trend in crimes against women. Data for recent years indicate that the incidence of molestation as well as torture of women is on the increase, and in 1992 these two offences together accounted for about 60 per cent of all reported crimes against women. Kidnapping and abduction and trafficking in women and girls are also serious crimes, constituting about 15 per cent of all crimes against women (table 79).

Although a large number of rape cases go unreported, rape accounts for about 15 per

Table 79. Reported incidence of various types of crime against women: 1990, 1991 and 1992

Type of crime	1990		1991		1992	
	Number	Percentage	Number	Percentage	Number	Percentage
Rape	10 068	14.6	10 425	14.0	11 734	14.7
Kidnapping and abduction	11 699	17.0	12 300	16.4	12 077	15.2
Dowry deaths	4 836	7.0	5 157	6.9	4 962	6.2
Torture	13 450	19.5	15 949	21.3	19 750	24.8
Molestation	20 194	29.3	20 611	27.6	20 385	25.6
Eve-teasing	8 620	12.5	10 283	13.8	10 751	13.5
Total	68 867	100.0	74 725	100.0	79 659	100.0

Source: National Crimes Records Bureau, cited in Central Statistical Organization, *Women and Men in India, 1995* (New Delhi, Ministry of Planning, Government of India, 1995).

cent of all reported crimes against women. Rape is the most violent, abrupt and physically and psychologically painful instance of male aggression, causing considerable trauma, humiliation, shame and guilt to the victims. As may be expected, most of the victims of rape are young. In all years from 1971 to 1992, more than 80 per cent of rape victims were under 30 years of age, and data for recent years indicate that a third of all rape victims are girls under 16 years of age.

The incidence of suicide among women is less than among men; available data for the period 1970-1991 indicate that suicides among women account for about 40 per cent of all reported suicide cases. The suicide rate or incidence of suicides per 100,000 persons is also significantly lower among females compared with males, although the rate for both males and females has been increasing since 1980 (table 81).

A classification of suicides in the country by cause and sex is given in table 81. The single most frequent cause of suicide among both males and females is suffering from a dreadful disease, which accounts for slightly more than a tenth of the suicides. Domestic quarrels (with parents-in-law or spouse) and emotional reasons (love affair) figure more prominently among women than men. Among "other causes" of suicide, dowry dispute accounted for about 4 per cent of suicides among women; while another approximately 15 per cent were recorded as "causes not known".

Table 80. Rape victims by age group: 1971-1992

Year	Age under 16 years		16 and under 30 years		30 years and over		All ages	
	Number	Percent-age	Number	Percent-age	Number	Percent-age	Number	Percent-age
1971	695	28.6	1 437	59.2	296	12.2	2 428	100.0
1976	692	17.8	2 576	66.2	625	16.0	3 893	100.0
1981	1 122	20.7	3 468	64.1	819	15.2	5 409	100.0
1986	1 261	15.9	5 305	66.7	1 386	17.4	7 952	100.0
1988	2 182	23.8	5 832	63.5	1 165	12.7	9 179	100.0
1989	2 334	23.9	5 646	57.9	1 772	18.2	9 752	100.0
1990	2 499	24.8	6 028	59.9	1 541	15.3	10 068	100.0
1991	3 729	33.8	5 377	48.8	1 919	17.4	11 025	100.0
1992	3 113	26.5	7 000	59.7	1 621	13.8	11 734	100.0

Source: National Crimes Record Bureau.

Table 81. Incidence of suicide and suicide rate by sex: 1970-1991

Year	Incidence of suicide						Suicide rate (per 100,000 persons)		
	Both sexes		Male		Female		Both sexes	Male	Female
	Number	Percent-age	Number	Percent-age	Number	Percent-age			
1970	48 428	100.0	28 846	59.6	19 582	40.4	7.9	9.2	6.5
1975	42 890	100.0	26 074	60.8	16 816	39.2	7.2	8.3	5.8
1980	41 663	100.0	24 188	58.1	17 475	41.9	6.3	6.9	5.4
1985	52 811	100.0	30 460	57.7	22 351	42.3	7.1	7.9	6.2
1990	73 911	100.0	43 451	58.8	30 460	41.2	8.9	10.2	7.6
1991	78 450	100.0	46 324	59.0	32 126	41.0	9.2	10.5	7.9

Source: National Crimes Records Bureau.

Table 82. Numerical and percentage distribution of suicides by cause and sex: 1981 and 1991

Causes of suicide	1981				1991			
	Male		Female		Male		Female	
	Number	Percent-age	Number	Percent-age	Number	Percent-age	Number	Percent-age
Failure in examination	517	2.2	327	2.0	833	1.8	547	1.7
Quarrel with parents-in-law	1 563	6.5	1 734	10.6	2 701	5.8	2 690	8.4
Quarrel with spouse	1 126	4.7	1 616	9.9	2 117	4.6	2 401	7.5
Poverty	734	3.1	442	2.7	1 310	2.8	637	2.0
Love affair	1 102	4.6	1 090	6.7	1 588	3.4	1 654	5.2
Insanity	845	3.5	598	3.7	1 643	3.5	1 026	3.2
Dispute over property	922	3.9	368	2.2	1 108	2.4	366	1.1
Suffering from dreadful disease	3 459	14.4	2 242	13.7	5 400	11.7	3 302	10.3
Unemployment	372	1.6	83	0.5	1 038	2.2	261	0.8
Bankruptcy or sudden change in economic status	230	1.0	63	0.4	735	1.6	172	0.5
Death of dear person	126	0.5	119	0.7	1 040	2.3	744	2.3
Fall in social reputation	275	1.2	135	0.8	244	0.5	175	0.5
Other causes	12 593	52.8	7 564	46.2	26 567	57.4	18 151	56.5
All causes	23 864	100.0	16 381	100.0	46 324	100.0	32 126	100.0

Source: National Crimes Records Bureau.

PART II
ANNEX TABLES

Table B.1 Outlays on different development activities in the Eighth Five-year Plan (1992-1997)

(Millions of rupees)

Development activities	Centre		States		Union territories		Total	
	Outlay	Percent-age	Outlay	Percent-age	Outlay	Percent-age	Outlay	Percent-age
Agriculture and allied activities	111 180.0	4.49	111 902.5	6.22	1 589.6	2.54	224 672.1	5.18
Percentage	*49.49*		*49.81*		*0.71*		*100.00*	
Rural development	241 700.0	9.75	102 132.6	5.67	421.0	0.67	344 253.6	7.93
Percentage	*70.21*		*29.67*		*0.12*		*100.00*	
Special area programmes	–	–	67 501.6	3.75	–	–	67 501.6	1.55
Percentage	*–*		*100.00*		*–*		*100.00*	
Irrigation and flood control	15 000.0	0.61	309 451.0	17.19	801.9	1.28	325 252.9	7.49
Percentage	*4.61*		*95.14*		*0.25*		*100.00*	
Energy	667 950.0	26.95	472 915.8	26.28	14 745.1	23.59	1 155 610.9	26.62
Percentage	*57.80*		*40.92*		*1.28*		*100.00*	
Industry and minerals	375 390.0	15.14	92 848.9	5.16	978.6	1.57	469 217.5	10.81
Percentage	*80.00*		*19.79*		*0.21*		*100.00*	
Transport	409 770.0	16.53	137 865.8	7.66	11 619.9	18.59	559 255.7	12.88
Percentage	*73.27*		*24.65*		*2.08*		*100.00*	
Communication	250 970.0	10.13	125.0	0.01	4.8	0.01	251 099.8	5.78
Percentage	*99.95*		*0.05*		*–*		*100.00*	
Science, technology and environment	51 390.0	2.07	38 428.8	2.14	598.1	0.96	90 416.9	2.08
Percentage	*56.84*		*42.50*		*0.66*		*100.00*	
General economic services	9 680.0	0.39	35 406.6	1.97	408.6	0.65	45 495.2	1.05
Percentage	*21.28*		*77.82*		*0.90*		*100.00*	
Social services	344 454.5	13.90	415 887.6	23.11	29 776.9	47.64	790 119.0	18.20
Percentage	*43.60*		*52.64*		*3.77*		*100.00*	
General services	1 165.5	0.05	15 383.8	0.85	1 555.5	2.49	18 104.8	0.42
Percentage	*6.44*		*84.97*		*8.59*		*100.00*	
Total	2 478 650.0	100.00	1 799 850.0	100.00	62 500.0	100.00	4 341 000.0	100.00
Percentage	*58.00*		*40.54*		*1.46*		*100.00*	

Source: Planning Commission, *Eighth Five-year Plan (1992-1997)* (New Delhi, 1992).

Table B.2 Outlays on different social services in the Eighth Five-year Plan (1992-1997)

(Millions of rupees)

Social services	Centre		States		Union territories		Total	
	Outlay	Percent-age	Outlay	Percent-age	Outlay	Percent-age	Outlay	Percent-age
General education	66 190.0	19.22	96 071.9	23.10	5 871.6	19.72	168 133.5	21.28
Percentage	*39.37*		*57.14*		*3.49*		*100.00*	
Technical education	8 240.0	2.39	18 046.6	4.34	1 577.2	5.30	27 863.8	3.53
Percentage	*29.57*		*64.77*		*5.66*		*100.00*	
Youth services	3 500.0	1.02	5 090.6	1.22	305.4	1.03	8 896.0	1.13
Percentage	*39.34*		*57.22*		*3.43*		*100.00*	
Art and culture	3 850.0	1.12	3 247.6	0.78	179.3	0.60	7 276.9	0.92
Percentage	*52.91*		*44.63*		*2.46*		*100.00*	
Medical and public health	18 000.0	5.23	53 077.7	12.76	4 681.5	15.72	75 759.2	9.59
Percentage	*23.76*		*70.06*		*6.18*		*100.00*	
Family welfare	65 000.0	18.87	–	–	–	–	65 000.0	8.23
Percentage	*100.00*						*100.00*	
Water supply and sanitation	59 680.0	17.33	98 472.6	23.68	8 957.7	30.08	167 110.3	21.15
Percentage	*35.71*		*58.93*		*5.36*		*100.00*	
Housing	16 913.5	4.91	34 090.8	8.20	1 725.9	5.80	52 730.2	6.67
Percentage	*32.08*		*64.65*		*3.27*		*100.00*	
Urban development	12 921.0	3.75	34 617.3	8.32	5 231.5	17.57	52 769.8	6.68
Percentage	*24.49*		*65.60*		*9.91*		*100.00*	
Information and publicity	1 990.5	0.58	2 156.8	0.52	67.8	0.23	4 215.1	0.53
Percentage	*47.22*		*51.17*		*1.61*		*100.00*	
Broadcasting	34 349.5	9.97	–	–	–	–	34 349.5	4.35
Percentage	*100.00*						*100.00*	
Welfare of scheduled castes, scheduled tribes and other backward classes	25 494.2	7.40	30 509.7	7.34	350.9	1.18	56.354.8	7.13
Percentage	*45.24*		*54.14*		*0.62*		*100.00*	
Labour and employment	4 495.8	1.31	8 399.8	2.02	244.1	0.82	13 139.7	1.66
Percentage	*34.22*		*63.93*		*1.86*		*100.00*	
Social welfare	23 730.0	6.89	14 677.2	3.53	144.9	0.49	38 552.1	4.88
Percentage	*61.55*		*38.07*		*0.38*		*100.00*	
Nutrition	100.0	0.03	17 424.0	4.19	439.1	1.47	17 963.1	2.27
Percentage	*0.56*		*97.00*		*2.44*		*100.00*	
Secretariat social services	–	–	5.0	–	–	–	5.0	–
Percentage			*100.00*				*100.00*	
Total	344 454.5	100.00	415 887.6	100.00	29 776.9	100.00	790 119.0	100.00

Source: Planning Commission, *Eighth Five-year Plan (1992-1997)* (New Delhi, 1992), pp. 61-62.

Table C.1 Sex ratio[a] at birth of registered live births in different states and union territories: 1956-1966

State/union territory	Year										
	1956	1957	1958	1959	1960	1961	1962	1963	1964	1965	1966
Group A											
Total[b]	109.9	109.9	109.9	109.9	109.9	109.9	111.1	112.4	111.1	112.4	112.4
Andhra Pradesh	107.5	107.5	107.5	107.5	107.5[c]	107.5	107.5	107.5	107.5	107.5	107.5
Delhi	108.7	111.1	108.7	108.7	108.7	108.7	108.7	111.1	111.1	113.6	111.1
Gujarat[d]	–	–	–	–	111.1	112.4	112.4	106.4	113.6	112.4	113.6
Haryana	–	–	–	–	–	–	–	–	–	–	112.0
Kerala	107.5	107.5	106.4	106.4	107.5	106.4	107.5	107.5	107.5	107.5	104.2
Madhya Pradesh	108.7	107.5	106.4	107.5	107.5	107.5	106.4	109.9	98.0	113.6	107.5
Madras (Tamil Nadu)	107.5	107.5	107.5	106.4	107.5	107.5	107.5	107.5	107.5	107.5	107.5
Maharashtra[d]	–	–	–	–	107.5	108.7	108.7	107.5	107.5	107.5	107.5
Mysore (Karnataka)	104.2	104.2	106.4	107.5	106.4	107.5	107.5	108.7	107.5	106.4	107.5
Orissa	107.5	107.5	107.5	107.5	107.5	106.4	107.5	107.5	106.4	106.4[e]	109.9[e]
Punjab	113.6	114.9	113.6	114.9	113.6	113.6	113.6	114.9	113.6	116.3	114.9
Uttar Pradesh	120.5	112.0	120.5	120.5	113.6	119.0	123.5	126.6	125.0	114.9	123.5
West Bengal	108.7	108.7	108.7	107.5	107.5	108.7	108.7	109.9	108.7	108.7	109.9
Group B											
Assam	106.4	101.0	103.1	107.5	104.2	103.1	107.5	107.5	109.9	113.6	104.2
Bihar	109.9	109.9	108.7	109.9	111.1	111.1	109.9	113.6	113.6	112.4	114.9
Chandigarh	–	–	–	–	–	–	–	–	–	–	112.4
Jammu and Kashmir	–	–	–	–	–	–	42.9	111.1	–	57.1	114.9
Rajasthan	112.0	122.0	–	117.6	120.5	119.0	122.0	112.4	120.5	116.3	116.3
Himachal Pradesh	113.6	–	112.4	112.4	113.6	113.6	119.0	113.6	112.4	116.3	114.9
Pondicherry	–	–	–	107.5	106.4	111.1	113.6	108.7	104.2	111.1	112.4
Andaman and Nicobar Islands	106.3	107.5	97.1	99.0	106.4	113.6	105.3	117.6	113.6	100.0	107.5
Goa, Daman and Diu	–	–	–	–	–	117.6	108.7	112.4	107.5	108.7	111.1
Lakshadweep	–	–	–	–	–	–	111.1	109.9[f]	113.6	101.0	104.2
Tripura	–	–	–	–	–	–	106.4	126.6	109.9	106.4	122.0
Dadra and Nagar Haveli	–	–	–	–	–	–	–	104.2[f]	97.1	104.2	101.0
Manipur	125.0	128.2	119.0	–	–	–	–	–	–	–	–

Source: Office of the Registrar General, India, *Vital Statistics of India,* reports for the years 1958, 1959, 1960, 1961, 1962, 1963-1964, 1965 and 1966.

[a] Number of males per 100 females.

[b] Sex ratio for total births refers to the births occurred in the states belonging to group A.

[c] Sex ratio at birth for Andhra Pradesh in 1960 excludes the number of births registered in Warangal Municipality.

[d] Maharashtra and Gujarat were constituents of Bombay before reorganization and Bombay had a sex ratio of 108 in 1956 and 109 for the years 1957, 1958 and 1959.

[e] Relating to urban areas only.

[f] Relating to rural areas only.

Table C.2 Age-specific death rates by gender: 1984

(Percentage)

Age group	Urban			Rural			Total		
	Male	Female	Total	Male	Female	Total	Male	Female	Total
0-4	22.6	23.8	23.2	44.2	48.2	46.2	39.5	43.0	41.3
5-9	1.6	2.1	1.9	4.1	5.3	4.7	3.6	4.6	4.1
10-14	1.2	1.3	1.3	1.7	2.2	2.0	1.6	2.0	1.8
15-19	1.6	2.2	1.9	2.1	3.0	2.6	2.0	2.8	2.4
20-24	2.1	2.8	2.5	3.0	4.2	3.6	2.8	3.9	3.4
25-29	2.3	2.2	2.3	2.9	4.4	3.7	2.8	3.8	3.3
30-34	2.2	2.3	2.3	3.5	3.8	3.7	3.2	3.5	3.4
35-39	4.2	2.5	3.4	4.5	4.7	4.6	4.4	4.2	4.3
40-44	6.5	4.2	5.4	6.6	5.7	6.2	6.6	5.4	6.0
45-49	9.9	5.1	7.5	10.1	6.8	8.5	10.0	6.5	8.3
50-54	13.7	9.9	11.8	16.1	11.1	13.6	15.6	10.9	13.3
55-59	21.9	14.4	18.2	20.8	15.8	18.3	21.0	15.5	18.3
60-64	35.3	26.9	31.1	36.3	31.3	33.8	36.1	30.4	33.3
65-69	51.5	38.9	45.2	50.4	42.6	46.5	50.6	.41.9	46.3
70+	104.2	93.1	98.7	112.4	106.0	109.2	110.8	103.4	107.1
All ages	8.8	8.3	8.6	13.5	14.0	13.8	12.4	12.8	12.6

Source: Office of the Registrar General, India, cited in Lyun Bennett, *Women, Poverty and Productivity in India* (World Bank, 1993).

Table C.3 Sex ratios (females per 100 males) by states and union territories: 1981

State/union territory	Urban	Rural	Total
Andhra Pradesh	984	948	975
Assam	917	768	901
Bihar	963	832	946
Gujarat	959	905	942
Haryana	876	849	870
Himachal Pradesh	989	795	973
Jammu and Kashmir	897	875	892
Karnataka	978	926	963
Kerala	1 034	1 021	1 032
Madhya Pradesh	956	884	941
Maharashtra	987	850	937
Manipur	971	969	971
Meghalaya	965	904	954
Negaland	899	688	863
Orissa	999	859	981
Punjab	884	865	879
Rajasthan	930	877	919
Sikkim	864	697	835
Tamil Nadu	987	956	977
Tripura	945	957	946
Uttar Pradesh	893	846	885
West Bengal	947	819	911
Andaman and Nicobar Islands	774	720	760
Arunachal Pradesh	881	629	862
Chandigarh	769	688	769
Dadra and Nagar Haveli	981	884	974
Delhi	810	808	808
Goa, Daman and Diu	1 013	919	981
Lakshadweep	986	963	975
Mizoram	928	893	919
Pondicherry	977	992	985
All India	951	902	933

Sources: Census of India, 1981, Series 1, India: Final Population Totals, Paper No. 1 of 1982, New Delhi: Office of the Registrar General, Ministry of Home Affairs, cited in Lynn Bennett, *Women, Poverty and Productivity in India* (World Bank, 1993).

Table C.4 Percentage distribution of male and female population by five-year age group: 1970-1992

Age group	1970 Male	1970 Female	1980 Male	1980 Female	1990 Male	1990 Female	1992 Male	1992 Female
0-4	15.0	15.2	13.3	13.2	13.3	13.2	13.2	13.0
5-9	14.2	14.3	12.7	12.6	11.7	11.7	11.9	11.8
10-14	12.5	12.1	12.2	12.0	12.1	11.6	11.2	11.0
15-19	9.2	8.7	11.3	11.1	11.0	10.2	10.9	10.2
20-24	7.5	8.1	9.5	9.3	9.4	9.6	9.7	9.9
25-29	7.2	7.6	7.4	7.2	7.9	8.1	8.1	8.1
30-34	6.6	7.1	6.0	6.3	7.0	7.0	7.0	7.1
35-39	6.1	6.0	5.5	5.8	5.8	5.9	6.0	6.1
40-44	5.5	5.2	5.2	5.4	5.0	5.0	5.0	5.0
45-49	4.4	4.0	4.5	4.5	4.3	4.4	4.4	4.5
50-54	3.9	3.7	3.9	3.8	3.7	3.7	3.7	3.7
55-59	2.5	2.4	2.9	2.8	3.1	3.0	3.1	3.1
60-64	2.4	2.5	2.3	2.4	2.1	2.3	2.2	2.3
65-69	1.3	1.3	1.5	1.6	1.8	2.0	1.7	1.9
70+	1.6	1.8	1.8	2.0	1.8	2.2	1.9	2.3
All ages	100.0	100.0	100.0	100.0	100.0	100.0	100.0	100.0

Source: Sample Registration System, reported in *Women and Men in India,* 1995 (New Delhi, Central Statistical Organization, Ministry of Planning, Government of India (1995)).

Table C.5 Gender differentials in performance at examinations conducted by the Central Board of Secondary Education in Delhi: 1971-1990

Year	Educational stage	Number of students appeared Both sexes	Male	Female	Number of students passed Both sexes	Male	Female	Percentage passed Both sexes	Male	Female
1971	Secondary	42 869	24 881	17 988	25 161	13 945	11 216	58.7	56.0	62.4
1976	Secondary	49 692	27 983	21 709	32 356	15 895	16 461	65.1	56.8	75.8
1981	Secondary	61 866	36 186	25 680	38 279	21 334	16 945	61.9	59.0	66.0
	Sr. Secondary	35 299	19 416	15 883	27 775	14 105	13 670	78.7	72.6	86.1
1986	Secondary	65 827	38 186	27 641	38 145	20 987	17 158	57.9	55.0	62.1
	Sr. Secondary	46 596	24 771	21 825	35 219	17 655	17 564	75.6	71.3	80.5
1987	Secondary	63 927	42 117	21 810	39 376	22 248	17 128	61.6	52.8	78.5
	Sr. Secondary	48 608	26 348	22 260	37 717	18 703	19 014	77.6	71.0	85.4
1988	Secondary	88 180	50 905	37 275	59 787	32 099	27 688	67.8	63.1	74.3
	Sr. Secondary	46 160	25 104	21 056	39 816	20 486	19 330	86.3	81.6	91.8
1989	Secondary	85 116	48 998	36 118	47 079	24 777	22 302	55.3	50.6	61.7
	Sr. Secondary	46 595	26 081	20 514	38 978	20 677	18 301	83.7	79.3	89.2
1990	Secondary	86 726	49 189	37 537	42 910	22 552	20 358	49.5	45.8	54.2
	Sr. Secondary	62 784	31 956	30 828	45 107	21 123	23 984	71.8	66.1	77.8

Source: Delhi Statistical Handbook, 1992.

Table C.6 Literacy rates of persons aged 7 years and over in urban and rural areas of major states, by sex: 1991

States	All areas			Urban areas			Rural areas			Urban/rural difference	
	Both sexes	Male	Fe-male	Both sexes	Male	Fe-male	Both sexes	Male	Fe-male	Male	Fe-male
Andhra Pradesh	44.1	55.1	32.7	66.4	75.9	56.4	35.7	47.3	23.9	28.6	32.5
Assam	52.9	61.9	43.0	79.4	84.4	73.3	49.3	58.7	39.2	25.7	34.1
Bihar	38.5	52.5	22.9	67.9	77.7	55.9	33.8	48.3	18.0	29.4	38.0
Gujarat	61.3	73.1	48.6	76.5	84.6	67.7	53.1	66.8	38.7	17.7	29.1
Haryana	55.9	69.1	40.5	73.7	82.0	64.1	49.9	64.8	32.5	17.2	31.6
Karnataka	56.0	67.3	44.3	74.2	82.0	65.7	47.7	60.3	34.8	21.7	31.0
Kerala	89.8	93.6	86.2	92.3	95.6	89.1	88.9	92.9	85.1	2.7	3.9
Madhya Pradesh	44.2	58.4	28.9	70.8	81.3	58.9	35.9	51.0	19.7	30.3	39.2
Maharashtra	64.9	76.6	52.3	79.2	86.4	70.9	55.5	69.7	41.0	16.7	29.9
Orissa	49.1	63.1	34.7	72.0	81.2	61.2	45.5	60.0	30.8	21.2	30.4
Punjab	58.5	65.7	50.4	72.1	77.3	66.1	52.8	60.7	43.9	16.6	22.3
Rajasthan	38.6	55.0	20.4	65.3	78.5	50.2	30.4	47.6	11.6	30.9	38.7
Tamil Nadu	62.7	73.8	51.3	78.0	86.1	69.6	54.6	67.2	41.8	18.9	27.8
Uttar Pradesh	41.6	55.7	25.3	61.0	70.0	50.4	36.7	52.1	19.0	17.9	31.4
West Bengal	57.7	67.8	46.6	75.3	81.2	68.3	50.5	62.1	38.1	19.1	30.1
India	52.2	64.1	39.3	73.1	81.1	64.1	44.7	57.9	30.6	23.2	33.4

Source: Office of the Registrar General, India, *Census of India, 1991: Final Population Totals,* Paper No. 2 of 1992.

Table C.7 Numerical distribution of the districts in 15 major states by level of rural female literacy rate: census of 1991

States	Literacy rate (percentage) of females aged 7 years and over									Total number of districts
	<15	15-24	25-34	35-44	45-54	55-64	65-74	75-84	85-94	
Andhra Pradesh	3	12	4	3						22
Assam		1	6	10	6					23
Bihar	14	24	4							42
Gujarat		2	3	9	4			1		19
Haryana		4	6	5	1					16
Karnataka		4	5	7	2	2				20
Kerala							1	5	8	14
Madhya Pradesh	14	23	6	2						45
Maharashtra		3	4	10	11		1			29
Orissa	2	4	4	1	2					13
Punjab			3	3	4	2				12
Rajasthan	23	4								27
Tamil Nadu			4	11	2	2		1		20
Uttar Pradesh	17	32	8	5	1					63
West Bengal		3	4	5	3	1				16
Total	73	116	61	71	36	7	2	7	8	381
Percentage distribution	19.2	30.4	16.0	18.6	9.4	1.8	0.5	1.8	2.1	100.0

Source: Office of the Registrar General, India, *Census of India, 1991: Final Population Totals,* Paper No. 2 of 1992.

Table C.8 Nutritional status of children (aged 1-5 years) in selected states by weight-for-age (percentage): 1975 and 1989

State	Year	Normal		Mild		Moderage		Severe	
		Both sexes	Girls	Both sexes	Girls	Both sexes	Girls	Both sexes	Girls
Kerala	1975	4.5	4.8	26.8	31.8	52.7	46.0	16.0	17.4
	1989	8.8	14.5	43.7	38.9	44.7	34.4	2.8	2.2
Tamil Nadu	1977-1979	4.5	2.5	28.4	27.7	53.4	49.6	13.7	20.2
	1989	7.1	7.0	41.0	38.5	46.6	49.7	5.3	4.8
Karnataka	1975	3.5	2.4	23.0	24.7	56.0	55.9	17.5	17.0
	1989	2.4	2.7	31.2	33.6	57.2	53.4	9.2	10.3
Andhra Pradesh	1975	2.6	3.1	21.7	21.7	54.0	51.2	21.7	24.0
	1989	4.8	5.8	34.0	32.1	50.7	52.7	10.5	9.4
Maharashtra	1975	1.2	2.0	19.4	19.0	53.0	47.0	26.2	32.0
	1989	5.4	6.4	30.1	34.2	55.3	50.3	9.2	9.1
Gujarat	1975	2.2	3.2	25.6	27.1	57.5	53.1	14.6	16.0
	1989	3.3	4.7	27.2	29.4	47.8	43.5	21.7	22.4
Orissa	1975	3.0	3.0	35.8	31.0	48.3	51.0	12.9	15.0
	1989	3.1	2.8	24.9	21.5	58.5	61.7	13.5	14.0
Average	1975	2.9	2.8	25.5	25.6	53.6	51.2	18.0	20.4
	1989	4.9	5.7	34.1	34.3	51.7	50.9	9.3	9.1

Source: National Nutrition Monitoring Board, cited in UNICEF, *Children and Women in India: A Situation Analysis, 1990* (New Delhi, 1991).

Table C.9 Percentage of live births during the four years preceding the 1992/93 National Family Health Survey by various maternal care indicators and state

State	Percentage receiving antenatal care	Percentage receiving two doses of tetanus toxoid vaccine[a]	Percentage receiving iron/folic tablets	Percentage of births delivered in medical institutions	Percentage of deliveries assisted by health professionals[b]
North					
Delhi	82.4	72.5	74.9	44.3	53.0
Haryana	72.7	63.3	59.9	16.7	30.3
Himachal Pradesh	76.0	47.4	71.7	16.0	25.6
Jammu Region of Jammu and Kashmir	79.5	68.9	70.7	21.9	31.2
Punjab	87.9	82.7	73.6	24.8	48.3
Rajasthan	31.2	28.3	29.2	11.6	21.8
Central					
Madhya Pradesh	52.1	42.8	44.3	15.9	30.0
Uttar Pradesh	44.7	37.4	29.5	11.2	17.2
East					
Bihar	36.8	30.7	21.4	12.1	19.0
Orissa	61.6	53.8	49.9	14.1	20.5
West Bengal	75.3	70.4	56.3	31.5	33.0
North-east					
Arunachal Pradesh	48.9	31.9	44.7	19.9	21.3
Assam	49.3	34.9	39.4	11.1	17.9
Manipur	63.4	48.0	35.5	23.0	40.4
Meghalaya	51.8	30.0	49.6	29.6	36.9
Mizoram	88.9	42.5	63.7	48.9	61.5
Nagaland	39.3	33.0	23.9	6.0	22.2
Tripura	64.9	58.7	53.2	30.7	33.5
West					
Goa	95.4	83.4	89.3	86.8	88.4
Gujarat	75.7	62.7	69.3	35.6	42.5
Maharashtra	82.7	71.0	70.6	43.9	53.2
South					
Andhra Pradesh	86.3	74.8	76.4	32.8	49.3
Karnataka	83.5	69.8	74.9	37.5	50.9
Kerala	97.3	89.8	91.2	87.8	89.7
Tamil Nadu	94.2	90.1	84.1	63.4	71.2
India	62.3	53.8	50.5	25.5	34.2

Source: International Institute for Population Sciences, *National Family Health Survey (MCH and Family Planning), India, 1992/93.*

[a] Including women who received more than two doses.
[b] Allopathic doctor or nurse/midwife.

93

Table C.10 Infant mortality rate in major states by sex and residence: 1991

Major states	All areas			Urban			Rural		
	Both sexes	Male	Female	Both sexes	Male	Female	Both sexes	Male	Female
Andhra Pradesh	73	76	70	56	65	47	77	78	75
Assam	81	88	74	43	49	36	83	90	76
Bihar	70	68	71	46	46	45	72	70	73
Gujarat	69	70	67	57	56	58	73	76	70
Haryana	68	69	67	50	48	51	73	74	71
Himachal Pradesh	74	81	67	38	49	27	76	82	69
Karnataka	77	82	72	47	51	43	87	91	82
Kerala	17	17	16	16	17	15	17	17	16
Madhya Pradesh	118	116	119	74	75	73	125	123	127
Maharashtra	60	60	59	38	42	33	70	69	70
Orissa	125	126	123	71	72	69	129	131	127
Punjab	53	55	51	40	41	38	58	60	56
Rajasthan	79	77	80	51	47	54	84	83	85
Tamil Nadu	57	60	54	42	43	40	65	69	61
Uttar Pradesh	98	95	100	74	70	77	102	99	105
West Bengal	71	72	69	47	44	49	76	79	73
India[a/]	81	81	80	53	53	52	87	87	87

Source: Office of the Registrar General, India, *Sample Registration System.*

[a/] Excluding Jammu and Kashmir.

Table C.11 Female literacy rate and female infant mortality rate in major states

Female literacy rate (1991) (percentage)	Female infant mortality rate					
	<20	50-59	60-69	70-79	80-89	90+
20-29				Bihar	Rajasthan	Madhya Pradesh Uttar Pradesh
30-39				Andhra Pradesh		Orissa
40-49			Gujarat Haryana West Bengal	Assam Karnataka		
50-59		Maharashtra Punjab Tamil Nadu	Himachal Pradesh			
80-89	Kerala					

Source: Office of the Registrar General, India, *Census of India, 1991,* Paper No. 2 of 1992; and *Sample Registration System.*

Note: Literacy rate is in respect of population aged 7 years and over.

Table C.12 Expectation of life at birth by sex and residence: 1970-1975 to 1986-1990

Residence	Period	Life expectancy at birth (years)			
		Both sexes	Male	Female	Male/female difference
India	1970-1975	49.8	50.5	49.0	1.5
	1976-1980	52.3	52.5	52.1	0.4
	1981-1985	55.6	55.4	55.7	−0.3
	1986-1990	57.9	57.7	58.1	−0.4
Urban areas	1970-1975	59.0	58.8	59.2	−0.4
	1976-1980	60.2	59.6	60.8	−1.2
	1981-1985	62.9	61.6	64.1	−2.5
	1986-1990	63.5	62.0	64.9	−2.9
Rural areas	1970-1975	48.0	48.9	47.1	1.8
	1976-1980	50.7	51.0	50.3	0.7
	1981-1985	53.8	54.0	53.6	0.4
	1986-1990	56.2	56.1	56.2	−0.1

Source: Office of the Registrar General, India, *Sample Registration System.*

Table D.1 Household composition and size: India, 1981

Household type	Urban		Rural		Total	
	Number	Percent-age	Number	Percent-age	Number	Percent-age
1. Single member	2 015 436	7.91	4 312 162	5.15	6 327 598	5.80
2. Head and spouse	1 324 214	5.20	4 106 841	4.91	5 431 055	4.98
3. Head and spouse with unmarried children:						
(i) 3-5 members	*6 705 531*	*26.33*	*19 959 960*	*23.86*	*26 665 491*	*24.43*
(ii) 6 members and above	*3 883 737*	*15.25*	*11 733 732*	*14.02*	*15 617 469*	*14.31*
(iii) Total	10 589 268	41.58	31 693 692	37.88	42 282 960	38.74
4. Head without spouse but with unmarried children:						
(i) 2-5 members	*947 602*	*3.72*	*3 398 118*	*4.06*	*4 345 720*	*3.98*
(ii) 6 members and above	*132 041*	*0.52*	*433 874*	*0.52*	*565 915*	*0.52*
(iii) Total	1 079 643	4.24	3 831 992	4.58	4 911 635	4.50
5. Head and spouse with or without unmarried children but with other relations who do not currently have spouse:						
(i) 3-5 members	*1 600 415*	*6.28*	*5 871 607*	*7.02*	*7 472 022*	*6.85*
(ii) 6 members and above	*2 331 540*	*9.15*	*8 187 627*	*9.79*	*10 519 167*	*9.64*
(iii) Total	3 931 955	15.43	14 059 234	16.81	17 991 189	16.49
6. Head without spouse but with other relations of whom only one has spouse:						
(i) 3-5 members	*313 888*	*1.23*	*1 276 909*	*1.53*	*1 590 797*	*1.46*
(ii) 6 members and above	*468 790*	*1.84*	*1 754 970*	*2.10*	*2 223 760*	*2.04*
(iii) Total	782 678	3.07	3 031 879	3.63	3 814 557	3.50
7. Head without spouse with or without un-married children but with other unmarried/ separated/divorced/widowed relations:						
(i) 2-5 members	*1 046 574*	*4.11*	*3 802 382*	*4.54*	*4 848 956*	*4.44*
(ii) 6 members and above	*260 855*	*1.02*	*1 017 699*	*1.22*	*1 278 554*	*1.17*
(iii) Total	1 307 429	5.13	4 820 081	5.76	6 127 510	5.61
8. Head and spouse with married son(s)/daughter(s) and spouses and or parents with or without other not currently married relation(s)/head without spouse but with at least two married sons/ daughters and spouse and/or parents with or without other not currently married relations:						
(i) 4-6 members	*765 216*	*3.00*	*3 563 154*	*4.26*	*4 328 370*	*3.97*
(ii) 7 members and above	*2 604 059*	*10.22*	*11 204 063*	*13.39*	*13 808 122*	*12.65*
(iii) Total	3 369 275	13.22	14 767 217	17.65	18 136 492	16.62
9. Head and spouse with married brother(s), sister(s) and their spouses with or without other relation(s) including married relation(s)/ head without spouse but with at least two married brothers/sisters and their spouses with or without other relations:						
(i) 4-6 members	*244 000*	*0.96*	*572 062*	*0.68*	*816 062*	*0.75*
(ii) 7 members and above	*736 640*	*2.89*	*2 380 857*	*2.85*	*3 117 497*	*2.86*
(iii) Total	980 640	3.85	2 952 919	3.53	3 933 559	3.61
10. Other households not covered elsewhere by size:						
(i) 2-5 members	*67 108*	*0.26*	*46 113*	*0.06*	*113 221*	*0.10*
(ii) 6 members and above	*24 383*	*0.10*	*45 594*	*0.05*	*69 977*	*0.06*
(iii) Total	91 491	0.36	91 707	0.11	183 198	0.16
11. Total number of households	25 472 029	100.00	83 667 724	100.00	109 139 753	100.00

Source: Census of India, 1981, Series 1, India, Part IV-A, *Social and Cultural Tables* (C-10, Household by composition and size) (Registrar General and Census Commissioner, India, 1990), pp. 4-9.

Table D.2 Percentage of female-headed households by urban and rural residence in states/union territories: 1981

State/union territory	All areas	Urban	Rural
Andhra Pradesh	11.51	10.24	11.88
Bihar	6.64	4.35	6.96
Gujarat	7.71	8.50	7.33
Haryana	6.32	6.99	6.09
Himachal Pradesh	16.32	13.30	16.65
Jammu and Kashmir	5.14	5.61	5.01
Karnataka	11.65	10.84	11.98
Kerala	19.37	20.46	19.13
Madhaya Pradesh	6.46	6.18	6.54
Maharashtra	9.07	7.81	9.76
Manipur	11.68	15.46	10.37
Meghalaya	22.23	21.05	22.50
Negaland	10.49	8.02	10.97
Orissa	8.34	7.28	8.49
Punjab	5.86	6.91	5.43
Rajasthan	5.27	5.39	5.23
Sikkim	9.45	8.00	9.76
Tripura	8.18	11.37	7.78
Uttar Pradesh	4.92	3.82	5.16
West Bengal	6.86	7.41	6.65
Andaman and Nicobar Islands	5.74	8.57	4.66
Arunachal Pradesh	7.54	5.80	7.69
Chandigarh	6.91	7.13	3.33
Dadra and Nagar Havelo	5.95	5.08	6.01
Delhi	5.81	5.93	3.80
Goa, Daman and Diu	23.25	18.34	25.63
Lakshadweep	34.36	37.53	31.72
Mizoram	10.91	15.29	9.44
India	8.08	7.64	8.21

Source: Office of the Registrar General India, *Census of India, 1981, Series 1, India,* Part IV-A, *Social and Cultural Tables.*

Table D.3 Singulate mean age at marriage by sex: 1961, 1971, 1981 and 1992/93

| State | 1961 census | | 1971 census | | 1981 census | | 1992/93 National Family Health Survey | | | | | |
| | | | | | | | Urban | | Rural | | Total | |
	Male	Female	Male	Female	Male	Female	Male	Female	Male	Female	Male	Female
North												
Delhi	23.3	18.7	24.0	20.0	24.3	20.5	24.4	21.0	24.1	19.0	24.3	20.9
Haryana	n.a.	n.a.	20.9	17.7	25.2	17.9	24.4	19.9	22.6	17.9	23.1	18.4
Himachal Pradesh	22.2	15.6	23.5	17.8	24.2	19.1	26.1	22.3	24.9	20.2	25.0	20.4
Jammu Region of Jammu and Kashmir	n.a.	n.a.	n.a.	n.a.	n.a.	n.a.	27.5	23.1	26.0	20.9	26.3	21.2
Punjab	22.6	17.5	24.1	20.1	25.0	21.1	25.5	21.7	24.6	20.9	24.8	21.1
Rajasthan	19.6	14.2	19.9	15.1	20.6	16.1	24.9	20.5	22.2	17.9	22.7	18.4
Central												
Madhya Pradesh	18.7	13.9	19.5	15.0	20.8	16.6	24.9	19.7	21.0	16.7	22.0	17.4
Uttar Pradesh	19.4	14.5	19.8	15.5	21.3	16.7	25.2	20.9	22.4	17.9	23.0	18.6
East												
Bihar	18.9	14.3	20.0	15.3	21.6	16.6	25.3	20.3	22.7	17.6	23.2	18.0
Orissa	21.9	16.4	22.7	17.3	24.3	19.1	27.2	21.8	25.3	20.4	25.6	20.7
West Bengal	24.3	15.9	24.6	18.0	26.0	19.3	27.6	21.8	25.0	18.1	25.9	19.2
North-east												
Arunachal Pradesh	n.a.	n.a.	25.6	19.6	n.a.	n.a.	25.6	19.8	24.8	20.0	24.9	20.0
Assam	25.9	18.6	25.8	18.7	n.a.	n.a.	29.2	23.0	27.7	21.4	27.9	21.6
Manipur	24.8	19.9	26.4	22.2	27.3	23.4	29.0	26.5	28.0	24.2	28.3	25.0
Meghalaya	n.a.	n.a.	25.5	20.2	26.0	21.0	27.1	23.3	24.6	20.6	25.1	21.2
Mizoram	n.a.	n.a.	n.a.	n.a.	n.a.	n.a.	28.5	24.0	26.9	21.4	27.8	22.9
Nagaland	26.2	22.2	27.8	24.0	29.0	24.8	26.3	19.0	25.7	22.8	25.8	22.7
Tripura	24.1	16.3	25.3	18.4	26.8	20.3	28.6	22.4	27.1	20.9	27.3	21.2
West												
Goa	27.1	20.9	n.a.	n.a.	28.5	23.0	30.7	25.0	30.5	25.2	30.6	25.1
Gujarat	21.7	17.1	22.4	18.5	23.3	19.6	24.8	20.6	23.5	20.0	23.9	20.2
Maharashtra	22.6	15.8	23.8	17.6	24.4	18.8	25.8	21.0	24.1	17.9	24.9	19.3
South												
Andhra Pradesh	22.3	15.2	22.8	16.3	23.1	17.3	25.6	20.3	22.8	17.3	23.6	18.1
Karnataka	24.7	16.4	25.2	17.9	26.0	19.3	26.9	20.8	25.6	19.0	26.1	19.6
Kerala	26.6	20.2	27.0	21.3	27.5	22.1	28.7	23.2	27.9	21.7	28.1	22.1
Tamil Nadu	25.3	18.4	26.1	19.6	26.1	20.3	27.3	21.3	25.9	20.0	26.4	20.5
India	21.9	15.9	22.6	17.2	23.5	18.4	26.3	21.5	24.4	19.3	25.0	20.0

Source: Office of the Registrar General, India, censuses of 1961, 1971 and 1981; and International Institute for Population Sciences, *National Family Health Survey (MCH and Family Planning), India, 1992/93.*

n.a. = not available.

Table D.4 Percentage of women married by specific exact age, current age and residence: 1992/93

Current age[a]	Percentage ever married before age:						Percentage never married
	13	15	18	20	22	25	
Urban							
15-19	1.8	5.5	..	..	..	..	78.2
20-24	3.9	10.9	32.6	52.5	..	..	31.8
25-29	5.9	16.1	40.9	59.9	73.5	86.5	8.9
30-34	6.8	16.9	46.2	65.1	78.1	89.3	3.1
35-39	8.9	20.8	51.9	69.8	81.5	91.4	1.7
40-44	11.9	25.6	56.1	73.6	85.0	92.9	1.9
45-49	13.6	27.9	59.2	77.2	87.4	94.4	1.6
20-49	7.4	17.9	44.9	63.7	75.8	84.6	11.0
25-49	8.6	20.2	49.0	67.4	79.7	90.1	4.1
Rural							
15-19	8.6	17.0	..	...	..	..	54.4
20-24	14.9	32.0	62.8	78.8	..	..	13.2
25-29	18.1	38.0	71.2	84.7	91.8	95.8	2.9
30-34	22.2	41.5	74.6	87.4	93.8	97.2	1.1
35-39	24.7	44.9	77.8	88.8	94.8	97.6	0.6
40-44	27.0	47.6	79.8	90.8	96.5	98.5	0.3
45-49	31.6	51.6	80.8	91.0	96.3	98.5	0.5
20-49	21.2	40.4	72.4	85.5	91.8	94.5	4.4
25-49	23.4	43.4	75.8	87.9	94.2	97.2	1.3
Total							
15-19	6.8	17.0	..	..	..	..	60.7
20-24	11.8	26.1	54.2	71.4	..	..	18.5
25-29	14.7	31.8	62.6	77.7	86.6	93.1	4.7
30-34	17.6	34.2	66.2	80.7	89.1	94.9	1.7
35-39	19.9	37.6	70.0	83.1	90.8	95.7	0.9
40-44	22.4	40.8	72.4	85.3	92.7	96.5	1.1
45-49	26.7	45.1	75.0	87.3	94.0	97.5	0.6
20-49	17.2	33.9	64.5	79.2	87.1	91.6	6.4
25-49	19.1	36.6	68.0	81.9	89.9	95.1	2.2

Source: International Institute for Population Sciences, *National Family Health Survey (MCH and Family Planning), India, 1992/93.*

[a] The current age groups include both never-married and ever-married women.
Two dots (. .) = not applicable.

Table D.5 Age-specific marital fertility rates in urban and rural areas: 1984-1991

Year	Age (years)													
	15-19		20-24		25-29		30-34		35-39		40-44		45-49	
	Urban	Rural	Urban	Rural	Urban	Rural	Urban	Rural	Urban	Rural	Urban	Rural	Urban	Rural
1984	0.2891	0.2249	0.3228	0.3178	0.2276	0.2635	0.1239	0.1850	0.0652	0.1149	0.0260	0.0602	0.0108	0.0302
1985	0.2970	0.2416	0.3305	0.3193	0.2039	0.2483	0.1153	0.1723	0.0523	0.0992	0.0231	0.0510	0.0102	0.0238
1986	0.2959	0.2482	0.3139	0.3165	0.2010	0.2459	0.1018	0.1626	0.0492	0.0966	0.0203	0.0493	0.0058	0.0215
1987	0.2992	0.2485	0.3251	0.3184	0.2086	0.2395	0.1032	0.1572	0.0537	0.0952	0.0214	0.0402	0.0065	0.0215
1988	0.3069	0.2521	0.3171	0.3205	0.1958	0.2384	0.0959	0.1520	0.0490	0.0913	0.0212	0.0439	0.0059	0.0173
1989	0.2880	0.2306	0.3218	0.3144	0.1953	0.2384	0.0892	0.1541	0.0468	0.0900	0.0201	0.0449	0.0065	0.0170
1990	0.2772	0.2448	0.3058	0.3109	0.1887	0.2268	0.0883	0.1433	0.0441	0.0885	0.0177	0.0404	0.0076	0.0176
1991	0.2836	0.2381	0.3163	0.3092	0.1825	0.2199	0.0881	0.1366	0.0407	0.0817	0.0169	0.0395	0.0064	0.0167

Source: Sample Registration System.

98

Table D.6 Fertility indicators by state and residence: 1990-1992

Region/state	Crude birth rate (per 1,000 population)			Total fertility rate (women 15-49 years)			Children ever born (women 40-49 years)		
	All areas	Urban	Rural	All areas	Urban	Rural	All areas	Urban	Rural
North									
Delhi	26.6	26.2	n.c.	3.02	3.00	n.c.	4.19	4.15	4.91
Haryana	32.9	26.7	35.1	3.99	3.14	4.32	5.21	4.35	5.51
Himachal Pradesh	28.2	20.2	29.0	2.97	2.03	3.07	4.42	3.41	4.54
Jammu Region of Jammu and Kashmir	27.9	21.2	29.3	3.13	2.13	3.36	5.05	3.89	5.37
Punjab	25.0	21.0	26.5	2.92	2.48	3.09	4.18	3.92	4.29
Rajasthan	27.0	22.3	28.1	3.63	2.77	3.87	5.00	4.14	5.22
Central									
Madhya Pradesh	31.6	27.1	32.9	3.90	3.27	4.11	5.22	4.58	5.42
Uttar Pradesh	35.9	28.5	37.9	4.82	3.58	5.19	5.97	5.18	6.19
East									
Bihar	32.1	27.5	32.9	4.00	3.25	4.14	5.23	4.59	5.36
Orissa	26.5	23.9	27.0	2.92	2.53	3.00	4.88	4.64	4.93
West Bengal	25.5	18.5	28.4	2.92	2.14	3.25	4.72	3.64	5.28
North-east									
Arunachal Pradesh	34.6	n.c.	34.6	4.25	n.c.	4.38	4.86	n.c.	4.88
Assam	30.4	23.2	31.4	3.53	2.53	3.68	5.74	4.16	6.01
Manipur	24.4	n.c.	25.5	2.76	n.c.	3.03	4.80	(4.51)	4.97
Meghalaya	31.9	n.c.	31.9	3.73	n.c.	3.80	4.92	(4.55)	5.03
Mizoram	20.8	n.c.	(19.6)	2.30	n.c.	(2.3)	4.26	(4.06)	4.43
Nagaland	31.3	n.c.	34.2	3.26	n.c.	3.60	4.16	(3.71)	4.28
Tripura	23.1	n.c.	24.5	2.67	n.c.	2.91	5.44	n.c.	5.70
West									
Goa	17.2	16.4	17.8	1.90	1.80	1.99	3.74	3.56	3.94
Gujarat	27.2	24.6	28.4	2.99	2.65	3.17	4.42	4.01	4.64
Maharashtra	26.3	24.2	27.9	2.86	2.54	3.12	4.25	3.94	4.53
South									
Andhra Pradesh	24.2	22.3	24.7	2.59	2.35	2.67	4.05	3.88	4.12
Karnataka	25.9	22.7	27.5	2.85	2.38	3.08	4.65	4.04	4.99
Kerala	19.6	18.0	20.3	2.00	1.78	2.09	3.65	3.31	3.82
Tamil Nadu	23.5	23.4	23.5	2.48	2.36	2.54	4.21	4.10	4.27
India	28.7	24.1	30.4	3.39	2.70	3.67	4.84	4.16	5.13

Source: International Institute for Population Sciences, *National Health Survey (MCH and Family Planning), India, 1992/93.*

n.c. = Not calculated.

( ) = Based on a few unweighted cases.

Table E.1 Percentage distribution of main workers by major industrial sector, sex and residence: censuses of 1981 and 1991

Industrial sector	Census year	India			Urban			Rural		
		Both sexes	Male	Female	Both sexes	Male	Female	Both sexes	Male	Female
Agriculture and allied	1981	68.8	65.7	81.3	13.0	11.7	23.1	83.4	81.7	89.1
activities	1991	66.8	62.7	80.7	13.4	12.1	22.3	82.3	79.8	89.5
Mining and quarrying	1981	0.6	0.6	0.3	1.1	1.1	0.7	0.5	0.5	0.3
	1991	0.6	0.7	0.3	1.1	1.2	0.7	0.5	0.5	0.3
Manufacturing, processing, servicing and repairs: (a) In household	1981	3.4	3.2	4.6	4.9	4.2	10.4	3.1	2.9	3.8
	1991	2.4	2.1	3.5	3.2	2.5	7.5	2.2	2.0	2.9
(b) Other than household	1981	7.8	8.9	3.6	24.8	26.0	14.6	3.4	3.8	2.1
	1991	7.8	8.9	3.9	22.1	23.2	14.1	3.6	4.0	2.3
Construction	1981	1.7	1.9	0.9	4.1	4.3	3.1	1.0	1.2	0.6
	1991	2.0	2.3	0.7	5.1	5.3	3.3	1.0	1.3	0.3
Trade and commerce	1981	6.3	7.4	2.0	19.9	21.3	8.9	2.8	3.3	1.1
	1991	7.4	9.0	2.3	21.9	23.7	10.0	3.3	4.0	1.1
Transport, storage	1981	2.8	3.4	0.4	9.1	10.0	2.2	1.1	1.4	0.1
and communication	1991	2.8	3.5	0.3	8.2	9.2	1.9	1.2	1.6	0.1
Other sources	1981	8.6	9.0	6.9	23.0	21.4	37.0	4.7	5.3	2.9
	1991	10.2	10.8	8.3	25.0	22.8	40.1	5.9	6.7	3.5
All sector	1981	100.0	100.0	100.0	100.0	100.0	100.0	100.0	100.0	100.0
	1991	100.0	100.0	100.0	100.0	100.0	100.0	100.0	100.0	100.0

Source: Office of the Registrar General, India, *Census of India, Series 1: Final Population Totals,* Paper No. 2 of 1992.

Note: The figures exclude Assam for 1981 and Jammu and Kashmir for 1991.

REFERENCES

Abouzahr, Carla, and Erica Royston (1991), *Maternal Mortality: A Global Fact-book* (Geneva, World Health Organization).

Alva, Margaret (1993), "Role of women leaders in community development: India", in Economic and Social Commission for Asia and the Pacific, *Women in Politics in Asia and the Pacific: Proceedings of the Seminar on the Participation of Women in Politics as an Aspect of Human Resources Development, 18-20 November 1992, Seoul* (New York, United Nations).

Banerjee, Nirmala (1985), *Women Workers in the Unorganized Sector* (Hyderabad, Sangam Books).

Bapat, Meera, and Nigel Crook (1988), "The quality of female employment: evidence from a study in Pune", *Economic and Political Weekly*, vol. 23, No. 31, 30 June.

Bennett, Lynn (1992), *Women, Poverty and Productivity in India*, EDI Seminar Paper No. 43 (Washington D.C., World Bank).

Bhatty, Z. (1975), "Muslim women in Uttar Pradesh: social mobility and direction", in A. de Souz, ed., *Women in Contemporary India* (Delhi, Manohar).

Caldwell, J.C., P.H. Reddy and P. Caldwell (1983), "Demographic change in rural South India" *Population Studies*, vol. 37, No. 2.

Central Statistical Organization (1995), *Women and Men in India, 1995* (New Delhi, Department of Statistics, Ministry of Planning, Government of India).

Chabra, Rami (1982), "Status of women in India", in Economic and Social Commission for Asia and the Pacific, *Population of India*, Country Monograph Series No. 10 (ST/ESCAP/220).

Dyson, Tim, and Mick Moore (1983). "On kinship structure, female autonomy and demographic behaviour in India", *Population and Development Review*, vol. 9, No. 1, March.

Economic and Social Commission for Asia and the Pacific (1982), *Population of India*, Country Monograph Series No. 10 (ST/ESCAP/220).

_____ (1996), *Socio-Economic Profile of SAARC Countries: A Statistical Analysis*, Statistical Profiles No. 1 (ST/ESCAP/1537).

Election Commission of India (1991), *Report of the Tenth General Election to the House of People of India 1991* (New Delhi).

Government of India (1990), *Employment: Past Trends and Prospects for 1990s* (New Delhi, Planning Commission).

_____ (1992), *Eight Five Year Plan (1992-1997)*, vol. I (New Delhi, Planning Commission).

_____ (1994), *Economic Survey, 1993/94* (New Delhi, Economic Division, Ministry of Finance).

_____ (1995), *Fourth World Conference on Women, Beijing, 1995: Country Report* (New Delhi, Department of Women and Child Development, Ministry of Human Resources Development).

_____ (1996), *Economic Survey, 1995/96* (New Delhi, Economic Division, Ministry of Finance).

Gulati L. (1975), "Occupational distribution of working women: an inter-state comparison", *Economic and Political Weekly*, vol. 10, No. 43.

Gupta, Devendra B, Alaka Basu and Biswanath Goldar (1995), *Population Change, Development and Women's Role and Status in India*, Economic and Social

Commission for Asia and the Pacific, Asian Population Studies Series No. 132 (ST/ESCAP/1592).

Institute of Social Sciences (1995), *A status Report on Participation of Women in Panchayat Raj* (New Delhi).

International Institute for Population Sciences (1995), *National Family Health Survey (MCH and Family Planning), India, 1992/93* (Mumbai, India).

Jose, A.V. (1988), "Agricultural wages in India", *Economic and Political Weekly*, 25 June.

Kadi, A.S. (1987), "Age at marriage in India", *Asia-Pacific Population Review*, vol. 2, No. 1, March.

Kapadia, K.M. (1966), *Marriage and Family in India* (Calcutta, Oxford University Press).

Krishnamurty, Sunanda (1988), "Wage differentials in agriculture by caste, sex and operations", *Economic and Political Weekly*, 10 December.

Kulkarni, P.M. and S. Rani (1995), "Recent fertility declines in China and India: a comparative view", *Asia-Pacific Population Journal*, vol. 10, No. 4, December.

Mohan, D. and A. Deopura (1996), *Accidental Deaths in India: A statistical Survey* (New Delhi, Centre for Bio-medical Engineering, Indian Institute of Technology).

Murty, N. (1982), "Reluctant patients: the women of India", *World Health Forum*, vol. 3, No. 3.

Nath, K. (1977), "Work participation and social change among rural women: a case study in Eastern Rajasthan, India".

National Institute of Urban Affairs (1988), "Extent and nature of economic participation of women in India", paper prepared for the Second Expert Group Meeting on the Role of Women in the Urban Informal Sector, New Delhi.

Nyrop, Richard F., ed. (1988), *India: A Country Study* (Washington D.C., Foreign Area Studies, The American University).

Office of the Registrar General, India (1982), *Census of India, 1981, Series I, India, Population Tables,* Paper No. 1 of 1982 (New Delhi).

_____ (1988), *Census of India, 1981.* Occasional Paper No. 7 of 1988, *Female Age at Marriage: An Analysis of the 1981 Census Data* (New Delhi).

_____ (1990), *Census of India, 1981, Series I, India,* Part IV-A, *Social and Cultural Tables (C-10, Households by Composition and Size)* (New Delhi).

_____ (1991), *Census of India, 1991, Series I, India,* Paper No. 3 of 1991.

_____ (1992), *Census of India, 1991, Series I, India: Final Population Totals,* Paper No. 2 of 1992 (New Delhi).

_____ (1992), *Survey of Census of Death (Rural)* (New Delhi).

_____ (1994), *Census Actuarial Report and SRS-based Abridged Life Tables, 1986-90,* Occasional Paper No. 1 of 1994 (New Delhi).

Ramachandran, K.V. and Vinayak A. Deshpande (1964), "The sex ratio at birth in India by regions". *Milbank Memorial Fund Quarterly,* vol. 42, No. 2 (Part I).

Rama, Rao G. (1996), "Feasibility of elementary education for all", *Productivity,* vol. 37, No. 3, October-December.

Retherford, Robert D. and J.R. Rele (1989), "A decomposition of recent fertility changes in South Asia", *Population and Development Review,* vol. 15, No. 4, pp. 739-747.

Selvaratnam, S. (1988), "Population and status of women", *Asia-Pacific Population Journal,* vol. 1, No. 2.

Singh, Prabhash Prasad (1991), *Women in India: A Statistical Panorama,* Women in South Asia Series No. 12 (New Delhi, Inter-India Publications).

The Economist Intelligence Unit (1996), *Country Profile: India and Nepal, 1995-96.*

United Nations (1994), *The Sex and Age Distribution of the World Population: The 1994 Revision* (New York, Department of Economic and Social Information and Policy Analysis (ST/ESA/ SER.A/144).

United Nations Educational, Scientific and Cultural Organization (1987), *Universal Primary Education for Girls: India* (Bangkok, UNESCO Principal Regional Office for Asia and the Pacific).

United Nations Children's Fund (1984), *An Analysis of the Situation of Children in India* (New York).

——— (1991), *Children and Women in India: A Situation Analysis, 1996* (New Delhi).

Visaria, Pravin and Anrudh K. Jain (1976), *Country Profile: India* (New York, Population Council).

World Bank (1996), *Improving Women's Health in India*, Development in Practice Series (Washington D.C).